Ghosts of the Blu

# Ghosts
## of the
# Bluegrass

James McCormick and Macy Wyatt

*Foreword by William Lynwood Montell*

THE UNIVERSITY PRESS OF KENTUCKY

Scholarly publisher for the Commonwealth,
serving Bellarmine University, Berea College, Centre
College of Kentucky, Eastern Kentucky University,
The Filson Historical Society, Georgetown College,
Kentucky Historical Society, Kentucky State University,
Morehead State University, Murray State University,
Northern Kentucky University, Transylvania University,
University of Kentucky, University of Louisville,
and Western Kentucky University.

*Editorial and Sales Offices:* The University Press of Kentucky
663 South Limestone Street, Lexington, Kentucky 40508-4008
www.kentuckypress.com

         13  12  11  10  09         5  4  3  2  1

Library of Congress Cataloging-in-Publication Data

McCormick, James, 1935–
    Ghosts of the bluegrass / James McCormick and Macy Wyatt ;
foreword by William Lynwood Montell.
        p.      cm.
    Includes bibliographical references and index.
    ISBN 978-0-8131-9237-6 (pbk. : alk. paper)
    1. Haunted places—Kentucky. 2. Ghosts—Kentucky.
3. Parapsychology—Kentucky. I. Wyatt, Macy, 1935– II. Title.
    BF1472.U6M397   2009
    133.109769—dc22

                        2009024161

This book is printed on acid-free recycled paper meeting
the requirements of the American National Standard
for Permanence in Paper for Printed Library Materials.

Manufactured in the United States of America.

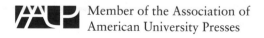 Member of the Association of
American University Presses

# Contents

# Illustrations

# Foreword

Children have always looked to parents and grandparents for insights into the mysteries surrounding them, especially to explain the unexplainable, since adults have told stories that contain beliefs and family traditions they gathered or experienced across the years. These rich stories and beliefs, some of which were brought into Kentucky during pioneer times, tell a lot about who we are, where our ancestors came from, and how we deal with the unknown in our lives.

It is no surprise that numerous persons in the Bluegrass and adjacent subregional areas of Kentucky enjoy a rich supply of ghost tales and premonition stories. Their ancestors, who occupied the flat land, rolling countryside, and adjacent hill and mountain terrain in early pioneer times, generated a storytelling legacy that continues in present times.

Regardless of geographical setting, traditional and present-day stories serve as ancestral and community-wide bonding agents. The introductory comments in these oral accounts provide an abundance of historical information. For example, ghost stories about haunted houses describe these old structures by identifying their location on the landscape, telling how many rooms were in them and who slept in which room, and describing the weird personality of Aunt Jane or Uncle Tom. Then suddenly here comes a ghostly being!

Not only houses provide havens for ghosts; these creatures often occupy old deserted roads, Civil War encounter sites, and old cemeteries—likely spots for ghostly visitations. It is not uncommon for ghost stories to provide social, cultural, and economic information about ancestors and ancestral times, as well as contemporary times—information that is not to be found on the formal pages of historical documents or public records.

Through stories, even those with ghostly themes, people are introduced to the names and actions of dead family members whom they never knew personally. Thus, they become acquainted with the ancestral dead as well as the living. At least that's the way it was in times past: stories could provide meaningful continuity between past and present generations. It is therefore important that stories such as those contained in this book be preserved for future generations, who may gather significant historical and personal information from them.

Technological improvements, accompanied by industrial and agricultural activities, became prominent in the Bluegrass and adjacent counties following World War II. These advancements, however, did not cause family and community storytellers to cease recalling with fondness the local stories passed along to them across the years. Tale swapping sessions were still popular on Saturday nights and Sunday afternoons until the advent of television, a device that regrettably turned children, even teenagers, away from the oral customs. Not all traditional activities died out, however; family and community social gatherings are still alive, as indicated in some of the stories included in this book.

Ghost stories included in the present book, along with those told and recorded elsewhere, describe the return of dead persons, typically as ghosts. Folklorists, along with certain oral historians, have actively been collecting these valuable oral accounts since the 1950s, and even earlier than that in some instances—for example, the notable folklorists Richard Dorson and Stith Thompson. The latter, a native of Willisburg, Washington County, Kentucky, researched ghost stories on national and international levels, resulting in a book series known as Motif-Index of Folk-Literature (Indiana University Press, 1955–1956). Dorson, author of numerous folklore books, founded the master's and doctoral degree programs in folklore and oral history at Indiana University in the 1950s; the program is still active and fruitful. As a doctoral student at Indiana University, I knew both Thompson and Dorson, and was influenced by their scholarly and creative abilities to produce books that focus on local people and their livelihood then and now.

As previously indicated, a ghost is a disembodied spirit, generally assumed to be that of a dead person. The stories in this book, as told orally, offer firsthand experiences with the return of the deceased as ghosts and describe significant family and community beliefs relevant to the Central Kentucky area. Thanks to Georgetown College professors James McCormick and Macy Wyatt, along with their students who recorded and/or received unembellished ghost stories, premonition beliefs, and related descriptive accounts from other individuals, Central Kentucky now has another book relevant to local life and culture, this one as portrayed by ghostly beings that still love the area and refuse to leave, even after death!

*William Lynwood Montell*
*Professor Emeritus of Folk Studies*
*Western Kentucky University*

# Acknowledgments

In January 1977, we taught a short-term class together at Georgetown College on interviewing techniques, using ghost stories as the vehicle for students to use in the interviews. At the time, we never dreamed the news would spread, causing other folks to consider us the "ghost busters of Central Kentucky" and to contact us to tell their own ghost stories. We are truly grateful to all of these persons. They are not named here, for some sent their stories anonymously and others did not want to be identified with ghosts!

We will identify and thank profusely those students enrolled in the class who braved the cold weather to collect the first stories that make up the nucleus of this collection. They are Belinda Rae Alexander, Martalea Allen, Meg Alloway, Deborah Kay Barnhill, Brenda Darlene Burns, Robert William Craig, David T. Gray, Tempa Harris, Esther Louise Houghton, Sharon Lee Kazee, James Ruben McIntyre, Judy Marlene Metcalfe, Frederick L. Moses, Martin R. Newberry, Pamela Sue Porter, Sara Carolyn Price, Peggy Ann Railey, Elaine Reynolds, David William Schiering, Howard Edwards Sellers III, Sheila Jo Short, Lisa Elizabeth Steely, and John Carroll Travis.

Our appreciation also goes to Tim Anderson, who supplied valuable photography and computer know-how and took a number of the photos in this volume. Eric Fruge of Georgetown College came across the intriguing photos and information about the Mystic 13, a group of female students at Georgetown College who studied the occult around 1917. We thank him for sharing his findings with us.

Initial editing and advice from a librarian's point of view were provided by Abigail Harris, who also gave valuable help in cutting down our verbiage. Mary McCormick aided us with her organizational skills and ability to keep details straight. We are grateful for their help in getting this collection into a manuscript form.

A chance conversation at an art exhibit with Mack McCormick, publicity manager of the University Press of Kentucky (and no relation to James), in which the collection was mentioned, ultimately led to our submitting the manuscript to the Press. Laura Sutton, acquisitions editor at the Press, has provided us valuable advice and encouragement. Our appreciation is given to these and others at the University Press of Kentucky who have helped our project along.

Last of all, but not least, we want to thank you, our readers, and we hope that these tales merit your approval.

# Introduction

Ghost stories have always been told. You may remember sitting on the front porch on a dark summer night, listening to someone tell ghost stories until you became overwhelmed with fear. Giving way to your fright, you ran home to the safety of a well-lit living room and comforting parents, but in the ensuing years, you have remembered the stories and perhaps even retold them.

Growing up in storytelling homes, we both have always collected stories for retelling but had never before collected them as a written record until beginning this project. During a January term at Georgetown College, we decided to team-teach a course on interviewing techniques, using ghost and death lore of Central Kentucky as the vehicle for teaching these skills. The students were to learn interviewing styles and various methods of transcribing and relating their interviews: first-person narrative, third-person retelling, dialogue style, and so on. Twenty-three students enrolled in the course and were given the instruction to go into the communities of Central Kentucky and collect ghost stories and death lore. It was a very cold January, but the students were enthusiastic and proved adept at achieving their goal. The class met daily to share the information gathered. Although the stories included in this anthology are primarily about ghosts, there are some that relate strictly to death lore. Our project began to snowball, and as stories accumulated, the need to compile this material led to the present anthology. It is interesting to note that this is not the first time students of Georgetown College showed an interest in the supernatural. From 1905 to 1917, an organization existed on campus whose members called themselves the "Mystic 13." It is not clear what the participants' specific interests were, but there are records acknowledging their existence.

Various styles of recording are found in this collection, because stories were gathered by many different individuals enrolled in the class, and the students were given the freedom to transcribe the stories in the manner they felt best represented the narrator. Most of the stories are presented as first-person narratives in paragraph form. In these, the compiler quotes the storyteller verbatim. Some compilers were more comfortable presenting the story in the third person by telling what the storyteller had said but not quoting directly. Other stories seemed to work best when recorded in a dialogue style, much like a play script. Students were encouraged to try different styles to see which worked best for getting the story across to the reader. After word got around that we were "ghost busters," we received several letters relating ghost stories and personal experiences. These have been printed in the form in which they were received unless editing for clarity or brevity was required. Our aim in editing was to preserve the flow and character of the interviews while making the stories concise and readable. We've shortened a few of the stories by omitting repetitive phrases and have not included every question and answer.

The belief in ghosts or spirits existing after physical death is not new. Ghosts have been discussed throughout history, and their characteristics seem to remain similar. One can find references to spirits appearing to people in the Bible, in 1 Samuel 28: 7–15, for example, when King Saul asks a medium to contact Samuel from the dead in order to consult him on military affairs, or in this passage from Job 4: 15–16, written between the mid sixth and the mid fourth centuries B.C.: "Then a spirit passed before my face; the hair of my flesh stood up. It stood still, but I could not discern the form thereof; an image was before mine eyes." Early instances of ghostly hauntings have been recorded in Egyptian hieroglyphics. The Egyptians believed that if a dead body was not properly cared for, then its spirit would leave the tomb and return to terrorize the living.[1]

Why ghosts appear remains a mystery. It may be that ghosts

come to comfort those who are left behind, maybe even to guard, protect, or warn them. Perhaps they come to inform about the circumstances of their deaths, sometimes even reenacting their deaths, or they may feel the need to complete a task. This raises the more fundamental question of why some people return as ghosts and others do not. We, the authors of this anthology, do not attempt to answer this question ourselves, but we have noticed that many ghosts act in repetitive ways, almost as if the person the ghost was in life is somehow caught in a loop after death, bound to repeat the same action over and over (as in "Image at the Window," chapter 1, or "Vanishing Hitchhiker," chapter 2). Other ghosts, however, are quite autonomous and inventive. (See "Blanche Eats the Ham," chapter 5.)

Some of the collected stories offer a natural cause for a mysterious haunt, like a white-faced cow in "Churchyard Ghost," chapter 7, or expose fake ghosts, as in "Sham Haunting," chapter 7. Others are obviously fictitious, designed to entertain. Most tellers of ghost stories, though, believe that the events occurred, and they claim actually to have experienced those events or to have been told the story by the person who directly experienced it. When a tale of this sort is related, one has to accept that the narrator believes the event took place. (Not all tellers believe in ghosts, however, and they often take pains to make sure that their audience knows this; see "Headless Woman," chapter 1, and "Vanishing Ghost," chapter 2.)

Charles Molin, author of *Ghosts, Spooks and Specters*,[2] points out that many ghost stories do not have a particularly interesting plot, since ghostly revelations are usually isolated incidents, and this will be evident in some of the stories found in this anthology. Our stories are unembellished. They are often brief and terse, and the language is that of the storyteller. We have eliminated hesitation and rambling in some cases, but otherwise the language and the grammatical construction are those of the teller. Many times you can sense the storyteller's embarrassment at relating a ghost story to a stranger or his/her "mike fright" at having it recorded. As you read, a vivid picture often emerges, as in the few paragraphs in which a tenant farmer tells of a ghost rocking in his rocking chair, of footsteps and other noises heard, and then ends with the simple, poignant statement: "We would've moved out sooner than we did if we'd had the money" ("A Persistent Ghost," chapter 4).

In compiling this anthology, we are making no attempt to convince people of the reality of ghosts, but neither are we negating the possibility of their existence or that of other such phenomena. As Charles Molin argues, with flawless logic, one can be confident that some ghosts are imaginary, "but to have imaginary people does not make all people imaginary, and to have imaginary ghosts does not make all ghosts imaginary."[3] What is most evident is that ghost stories are part of our heritage and must be treated as such. Much as you might pass down your great-grandmother's wedding dress, people pass down stories, and they reflect both temporary cultural preoccupations and perennial interests.

Some of the ghost stories in this anthology are purportedly based on historical events. In their book *Haunted Heritage*,[4] Michael Norman and Beth Scott describe several such ghost stories and point out that it is not necessary to believe the events described in ghost stories actually occurred; rather, it is enough that *the narrator* believes the events took place. This is also true of some of the stories found in this anthology.

One example of how a ghost story can shed light on a historical period is *A Short Statement Concerning the Strange Visitation Which During Twenty Nine Years, Afflicted THE FAMILY OF JOHN HORRELL, Living near St. Anthony's Church, Long Lick, Breckinridge Co., Ky.*, a book published in the late nineteenth century in Kentucky, and here, in chapter 11, reprinted for the first time. In *A Short Statement* we can clearly discern the racism that was so prevalent during the era in which the story takes place. Is it a "true" story? We don't know if the events it narrates happened as reported, but, as a story, it is as much a part of our heritage as any physical artifact, even though we wish the racial insinuations were not.

Storytelling differs from history in that it is more personalized. Ghost and death lore reflect our speculations about death, life beyond death, and the fear of death. Regardless of our own personal beliefs about ghosts, death, and the afterlife, we were continually impressed with the sincerity of most informants in recounting their experiences. Having said that, however, we note that not all ghost stories are taken seriously even by the tellers, as in the story of a ghost who rises to chase anyone who yells "Pabst Blue Ribbon" three times across her grave ("This Ghost Will Chase You," chapter 1). Maybe she was a Miller fan!

Many of the stories appear to be regional. A similar story is told by several persons in the same area, usually with slight modification. For example, in Central Kentucky we heard numerous stories that took place on college campuses, and, not surprisingly, many of these occurred on the Georgetown College campus. Other stories are more than just regional; they are universal. The "vanishing hitchhiker" is one such universal type that is told around the world;[5] it is found in this anthology in stories that recount a mysterious female hitch-hiker who is seen or given a ride and subsequently is discovered to have been killed along that same highway. (See "Hitchhiker Ghost," "Taxi Rider," and "Vanishing Hitchhiker," in chapter 2.)

Originally we planned to limit our collection of ghost and death lore to the Bluegrass or Central Kentucky region. We soon came to realize that, even though the contributors were residents of Central Kentucky, some of their stories related to a place of birth or to former residences outside the Bluegrass. Several stories are from other states, reflecting our mobile society. Some stories come from other parts of Kentucky. Thus we decided on the title *Ghosts of the Bluegrass*.

The Bluegrass region is usually defined as the city of Lexing-ton, which is in Fayette County, and the surrounding counties of Franklin, Scott, Bourbon, Madison, Clark, Jessamine, and Wood-ford. Some might include other nearby counties such as Harrison, Mercer, and Boyle. This part of the state is more urban than some other regions. The land is flat to rolling, and this is where large thor-oughbred horse farms are found. Many early settlers of the Central Kentucky region were people of means coming from Virginia who could afford to buy the rich farmland.

Central Kentucky is different from Eastern Kentucky, which is a more isolated mountainous area in the foothills of the Appalachian chain. Although stories were told in Central Kentucky, just as they are everywhere people gather, much more emphasis has been placed on collecting folklore, including songs, crafts, and stories, in the Appalachians, since the geographical isolation caused folk traditions to remain relatively unchanged from generation to generation. Because of Central Kentucky's flatter land, travel was easier, and there was more melding of tales and traditions as people from various parts of the country (and immigrants from other countries) arrived and settled, or just passed through on their way to other destinations, and so the stories that were told were influenced by stories from these newcomers or visitors. The geographic differences make the collector less likely to find older stories, such as the "Jack" tales, which are told in Eastern Kentucky, but stories of supernatural happenings in Central Kentucky were shared and still abound.

Although we started this project hoping to capture what we had assumed would be quickly fading memories of ghosts, goblins, and (mostly rural) superstitions, we found that the stories are still alive and well even in our modern scientific world, and that ghost and death lore, far from being a dying folk style, is still a part of contemporary society not limited by race, creed, class, or rural/urban status. A second, but no less important, goal was to stimulate questions in the reader's mind, regardless of his or her predominant skepticism or prior belief in ghosts. If you don't believe in ghosts, we hope that the stories presented here will make you examine why you are skeptical. And conversely, if you do believe, we invite you to consider some of the alternate opinions expressed by certain storytellers. Human nature seems to crave knowledge that is seemingly unknowable; perhaps people look to the supernatural when there do not seem to be satisfactory answers to their questions in the everyday "real" world. Regardless of the reason, this interest has led people to the séance table, to fortune-tellers, and to haunted houses. It also leads people to read books such as this collection of ghost stories and has spawned an entire segment of the entertainment industry as well, which brings horror fiction and horror movies to a wide and eager audience.[6] Even though people may never have definitive answers to the questions they raise, the pursuit of the answers is exciting and stimulating, albeit sometimes frightening. We hope you enjoy this collection, whether as entertainment, or information, or perhaps as both.

## Notes

1. Stuart A. Kallen, *Ghosts* (Farmington Hills, Mich.: Lucent Books, 2004), 14–29.

2. Charles Molin, *Ghosts, Spooks and Specters* (New York: David White, 1967), 7.

3. Ibid.

4. Michael Norman and Beth Scott, *Haunted Heritage* (New York: Tom Doherty Associates, 2002), 15–16.

5. For an example of a "vanishing hitchhiker" story from the Philippines, see "Mysterious Woman at the Intersection," Your Ghost Stories, http://www.yourghoststories.com/real-ghost-story.php?story=1379 (accessed December 17, 2008).

6. The interest in ghost and death lore has also created a strong following for supernatural nonfiction written for a mainstream audience. The extreme popularity of Sylvia Browne's books, as well as those by James van Praagh, John Edward, Hans Holzer, and others, attests to the immense number of readers who are interested in such topics.

*Chapter 1*

# Unfinished Business

We begin with stories depicting ghosts who seem to return to complete unfinished business. Some are quiet, and some are disruptive. They may or may not materialize. They may make themselves known by their actions, such as moving or rearranging objects, making the sound of footsteps, or turning lights on and off. They usually appear at the place where the unfinished business occurred (or didn't occur!).

Why do some people become ghosts when they die, while others do not? Unfinished business is one possible answer to this question. Perhaps the circumstances of an individual's life or death affect his or her afterlife, or maybe she is just expressing some sort of dissatisfaction over the way she was treated while alive. It may be that the person who becomes a ghost is extremely attached to a particular object, person, or place, or may even wish to avenge his own death.

It is interesting to note that certain locales seem to generate more ghost stories than others. Based on her personal experiences, ghost researcher Katherine Ramsland maintains that the belief in ghosts is more prevalent in the South than in other parts of the United States: "I had found more people in the South than anywhere else who could speak easily on the topic of ghosts. Ghosts are to the South as works of art are to Italy: They're part of daily life and you find them everywhere."[1] This could possibly account for our finding, as mentioned in the introduction to this anthology, that nearly everyone our researchers contacted had a ghost story to tell, even if they, personally, had not experienced a ghost.

## Miss Lucy

Well, I don't believe any of the stories I have been told about this house, but I will say my husband believed there was a ghost. He was a big Irishman who would believe in anything if it was fantastic enough. The stories he has told me are pretty fantastic.

All I can say is that the ghost's name is supposed to be Miss Lucy. She was one of the two Ashmore sisters that lived in this house many years ago. Anytime she has been spotted, she has been wearing a black dress and carrying a parasol. She never stays in one place very long.

*Female, age 40, Woodford County*

## Miss Lucy Appears to an Earlier Resident

I have never really seen the ghost. But I will say that sometimes I could almost feel the presence of someone else in the room with me when I was supposedly alone.

*Interviewer: Have you ever had anything out of the ordinary happen to you or your family? Have you ever talked to anybody who has seen Miss Lucy?*

There are two interesting incidents that happened to my children and me. When Tricia was about five, I guess, she came into my bedroom complaining that she couldn't sleep. My husband was away, and I was in this big house alone with the children. When I asked her why she couldn't sleep, she simply replied, "There's a lady in my room." I told her to sleep with me and that everything would be all right. She wasn't scared at all, just annoyed with this lady.

*Interviewer: Had Tricia ever been told about the ghost?*

Never. Since I first heard the stories about the ghost, I made sure the children never heard anything about it. Tricia never mentioned the incident again, and to this day she doesn't even remember it when I tell her about it.

The other time was when Billy was about four. Tricia, Billy, and I were all sleeping in the room we used upstairs for a study one night. I wasn't sleeping, but I was trying to get the children to go to sleep because they were restless. Again my husband was away, and I had some cleaning to do after the children went to sleep. Anyway, I almost had them asleep when Billy looked up and said, "Mama? Look at that lady!" I told him to go to sleep, but he kept on, "Look, Mama! Look, Mama!" I was too scared to turn around. I wasn't about to look.

*Interviewer: How did the children describe the lady?*

Tricia said she was a very pretty old woman, dressed in black with a small umbrella. Billy never did say what she looked like. It is strange, though, that the stories told about Miss Lucy always had her dressed in a black dress carrying a parasol.

*Interviewer: How does everyone know her name?*

The ghost has been talked about all over town for years. Everyone knows her as Miss Lucy. Her real name was Miss Lucy Ashmore, one of the two sisters that lived in the house.

*Female, age unknown, Woodford County*

## Headless Woman

I don't believe in ghosts and all that nonsense, but you always hear it, especially when you're young. People were always telling them [ghost stories] to us just to try to scare my sister and me, but since I didn't believe in them, I didn't pay too much attention to them, so I don't remember but one.

This was supposed to have happened not far from the house I lived in as a child, which was out in the country. People would talk of seeing a headless woman walking up and down the road that led into town. She was dressed all in white, and the long dress was sort of a shiny white. She was only seen at night, especially if it was really dark, like when the clouds cover the sky and when you can't see the moon or stars. She would just be walking up and down the road.

*Interviewer: Nobody knew who she had been?*

There was some woman who was supposed to have been hung in a house around that area, but I don't know for sure, and I don't think anybody else did either.

*Interviewer: Did you ever see her yourself, or did one of your sisters?*

Nobody in my family, including me, ever saw her. People just told us about it.

*Female, age 70, Woodford County*

## Ghost with a Sense of Humor

This story happened in a two-story house in Harrison County. The house was built around 1820. We had not been living in the house very long when one evening, while sitting in the den watching television, we suddenly heard distinct footsteps going up the stairs. My husband got up to see who had gone up the stairs but found no one. The whole family was sitting in the den, including the pets. This happened on several occasions during the period we lived in the house, and we could never account for the sound.

In the same house, various lights would come on during the night while everyone was sleeping. It was never the same light. My son claimed something or someone jerked the covers off of him while he slept, waking him up. My husband said he felt like someone hit him on the head with what felt like an empty plastic bottle while he was sleeping. In case you are wondering, I was sound asleep while all of this was occurring.

As mentioned, we had a cat and a dog while living in that house. Our cat, while walking through the house, would suddenly stop, jump straight up in the air with its hair sticking straight up, and then run out of the room. There would be nothing that we could see that might have frightened the cat. When we moved away from the house, the cat never acted that way again.

*Female, age 35, Harrison County*

*Animals are perceived as being naturally more perceptive and sensitive to the supernatural. Since ghosts are utterly primitive, animals—which are less contaminated by civilization and therefore closer to nature—are thought to be able to sense a ghost even when our human senses cannot detect any changes in our surroundings. In ghost lore, a reaction from an animal functions as proof that more than likely there really is "something there," that it is not just a notion in the head of a superstitious person. Since dogs and cats are our most common animal companions, they figure most often in stories involving animal perception of spirits, but horses have been known to shy in the presence of ghosts, and there have undoubtedly been instances of spirit perception by other animals. Likewise, there are recorded sightings of animals who are ghosts themselves.*

## Ghost Appears to a Friend

This guy was about fifteen years old, and he had a history of problems. It was mental, like he wasn't altogether there. So one morning his parents found him out in the field with a bullet in his head; he had shot himself. He left a note for a friend of his saying the reason he had shot himself was he wanted to be in heaven away from those who were after him. He also told the friend he would come back and tell him what heaven was like.

One night his friend was sleeping, and the guy who shot himself came in the room and told his friend he really liked heaven, and he was happy there away from those who were after him. So about a week or two later, the friend shot himself too. He left a note saying he wanted to be with his friend in heaven, and also he thought someone was after him and that they were going to kill him and his brother, too. So he was going to shoot himself before they killed him. This boy's mother said the brother wasn't scared of anyone who came after him, and he is still living.

*Female, age 25, Boyle County*

## Image at the Window

I was born in this particular house. It was a great big house, a farmhouse, brick, painted white, two-story, basement and all that. But the old lady that owned it before my father bought it in 1908—for about her last ten, fifteen years—she sat at this front window and looked out. She couldn't get around. She couldn't walk, but she sat in this chair, day after day, in a rocking chair, and looked out the window.

She died, and they sold the farm, and my father bought it. Every night as he drove his old Model T home and pulled in the driveway, his light would go across that window, and there would be the old lady sitting in the chair. She wouldn't be there at any other time, only when the lights were out in the house and you'd shine a strong flashlight or car light across the window. They bulldozed it down, but the house was there until 1946–1947.

We had a theory about the image, sort of like a photographic effect. Say that if you take an image and you place that image on a transparent surface, every day, year after year, then it is bound to have some effect on the glass or transparent surface. Maybe over the years, she did something to the glass. Or it could have been she was there—she wasn't through doing her thing. A person has to make up their own mind. My father changed the glass one time, but it didn't get rid of her. The second time he changed it, the whole window casing was replaced, and that finally got rid of her. Around 1935, she disappeared.

*Female, age 52, Scott County*

*It is a natural human tendency to want to find logical reasons for seemingly unexplainable happenings. In the above story, an intriguing physical explanation of what might have caused the appearance of a ghostly image is attempted. However, the teller argues against her own explanation when she tells us that the image was still there after her father replaced the glass. In the end, the teller cannot come up with a reasonable explanation, but even so, interestingly, she still never once calls the image a "ghost."*

## Lantern on the Tracks

The name of the road is the Old Train Road, and the legend is that about, oh, fifty years ago, it was a railroad track and now it is a road. One night, someone carried a lantern—I believe they were out hunting—and was killed by the train. The train dragged the lantern down the track, and they never did find it.

Anyway, on certain nights with certain conditions, usually when it's very humid, you can walk down the road and the light will actually come up to you. I know this for a fact because one night when we were out coon hunting, I got separated. I was tracking one of the dogs down 'cause we had two dogs and they had taken different tracks. So I was following the Old Train Road 'cause that led to the Baker Road, where our truck was parked. I knew this, you know. So anyway I see this light was coming, meeting me, and it was jerking like someone was walking. I figured it was just someone else, you know, in our same party, 'cause there were about ten of us men out hunting. So, anyway, it got about twenty foot from me, and I started calling out names. As the light got within three foot of me, it went out. It was a moonlit night, and there was just nothing there . . . and neither was I in about two seconds!

*Male, age 20, Scott County*

## Hands at the Window

Near Frankfort there's an old bridge. They tore down the bridge and put in a new bridge because the old one was dangerous. There was a story about a man who was driving across the bridge and ran out of gas. He went to get gas, but he never made it to the gas station. They found his body at the bottom in the creek.

His body was intact, except both his hands were cut off! Years later a woman was coming across the bridge, and she ran out of gas at the very same spot. She decided she would wait in the car because she didn't want to get out and walk the dark roads. She locked herself in the car, rolled up the windows, and sat there and waited. She was sitting there waiting for somebody to help her, when she heard a "rap, rap, rap." She looked up and there were two hands, no body, just two hands pecking on the windows. Just sitting there pecking on the windows. So now nobody runs out of gas on that road!

*Male, age 45, Franklin County*

# Gypsy Ghost

There's a Gypsy Queen buried in our cemetery here [in Georgetown]. Once a year there's a pilgrimage here by the gypsies to this cemetery. They come in the summer and they stay right in the cemetery for three or four days. Supposedly this queen comes out of her coffin while they are there. This has gone on for years. In fact, it's a ritual they go through. They don't like you watching them. They chased us out when we were kids.

*Male, age 30–40, Scott County*

# Voices from the Grave

This happened in "Hinterland." There was a man who passed away. He was supposed to be an odd character. At that time, cemeteries rounded off the graves. They had a caretaker come there with sheep shears and clean off the tops, the grass and all. He would just straddle that grave. The caretaker lived on the other side of town, and he was very arthritic, all crippled up. One day when he was down there mowing the grass of the odd character's grave, a voice said to him, "Get up off of me."

He looked all around, and he couldn't see a thing. He got on back to mowing the grass on the mound over the grave. This voice said, "I told you to get up off of me!"

He kept looking and couldn't see a thing. He just heard that voice. So he went back to his cutting. Then this voice says, "How many times do I have to tell you?" So that guy left so fast, he left his crutches by the grave. He walked for three miles, and you know what? He never was crippled anymore!

*Male, age late 60s, Scott County*

# Peddler Returns

My grandfather told me this story, which took place in the 1930s. He used to stay with this family named Webster.

Back in the 1800s or something like that, before that family moved there, an old peddler used to come around. In those days they carried gold instead of paper money. The family that lived in the house killed the peddler for his gold and buried him in the garden.

My grandfather said that on certain nights during the week, you could see this peddler come up out of the ground. He said he'd be in the form of a little short black figure carrying a lantern. Many a night, my grandfather said, he'd stand and look out the window and watch the peddler come up out of the ground.

The peddler would run! He'd come running toward the house, and he would run into the house and slam the door behind him! Then he'd run from room to room, slamming doors and screaming, because the people who had lived there had killed him and had chased him through the house. He would run through the house, slamming doors and screaming at the top of his lungs, carrying his lantern.

My grandfather said the guy would then leave the house and run down the road. His neighbors down the road had some dogs, and when they saw the thing coming they ran up to it, barking and howling. But when the hot air from the spirit would hit the dogs in the face, they would scream, yelp, and run back to their house.

Grandfather said it had done it so much that they had gotten used to it, and they would sit there, the lady and her kids, while it ran around through the house slamming the doors!

*Male, age 20, Scott County*

*The spirit in the above story is very unusual in that he gives off hot air that frightens the dogs. (For another "hot air" story, see "The Ghostly White Dog," chapter 4.)*

## Lady with a Knife

This story was told to scare the kids around my hometown, but it actually did happen. There was a woman who had gone insane before she died, and she would wander. She lived near a church. It was a spooky kind of building set back in the trees.

Many years after her death, a man got caught in a storm. Since he was on horseback, he was forced to find shelter at the nearest available place. Lightning lit up the sky and he saw the old church, so he ran into it. When the lightning lit up the sky again, he saw this woman standing in the storm holding a corn knife, which is about two and a half feet long. Again the lightning lit the scene, and he saw her coming toward him with that huge knife in her hand, and, storm or no storm, he ran away. The church is the Cosby Methodist Church in Hart County.

*Male, approximately 40, Scott County*

## Ghostly Revenge

There were two neighbors named Clawson and Ingram on my street when I was a boy. They had a little ditch that took care of the water running on their property. The ditch stopped up and ran over onto Ingram's property. Ingram said that he was going to fix it so that the water ran into a stream over there. Clawson said, "That's my side of the road, and if you touch it, I'll kill you."

But Ingram complained that he couldn't get into his driveway. So he went to see the judge, and the judge said that it was Ingram's property, and he could do anything he wanted. Ingram went and told Clawson what the judge had said. But Clawson still said he'd kill him if he touched the ditch. So Ingram started to dig, and Clawson shot him with a shotgun. Clawson tried to get away but failed. He went to jail, and he got out on parole. He came back home where his wife was keeping the farm.

Ingram had a little boy who swore that, when he became a man, he would kill the man who had shot his daddy. This boy, after he grew up, came home drunk one Sunday and died in a house fire. Soon afterward, Clawson was in his barn one windy night, and he could sense that the barn was going to be torn apart. Well, he started to run to the house, but when he was halfway there the barn blew apart and a piece of wood flew out, hit him, and killed him. People said that Ingram's son had come back from the dead and gotten his revenge.

*Male, age 84, and his wife, Scott County*

*In ghost stories, the storyteller sometimes becomes an omniscient narrator, relating "facts" that he could not possibly know or describing the thoughts of a character. Since storytellers want people to believe their stories, the question arises: why tell a story in a way that undercuts its believability? Does the storyteller actually doubt the story at some level and want to subtly hint at that? Or does he simply embellish the story to make it sound more dramatic, and offer proofs of its veracity by using literary devices such as telling the listener what thoughts were running through a character's mind? In this story, the narrators assume that the death of Clawson is a revenge killing, since Ingram's son had sworn to avenge his father's death, and so they explain Clawson's actions in a way that fits the facts as they understand them. Thus they can say that "Clawson sensed danger"—and his actions seem to back up this assumption—when in reality the narrators have no way of knowing why Clawson acted as he did during the last moments of his life.*

## David Shelly's Ghost

Harrison County's most famous ghost story is that of David Shelly. David and his friends were out fishing one night and took along a few extra jugs of whiskey and got drunk. When they came in, they had the fish yet to clean and they were hungry, so one of the men suggested that they would surely like to have something to eat. David said, "Well, my wife will fix you something to eat."

The men said, "Naw, she won't."

David said, "Yes, she will." So they went home to David's small shack of a house back an off-road, and David told his wife to fix all the men something to eat. Well, she didn't want to, so she went on into the bedroom. The men, drunk as they were, just laid down in the house in various places and dozed off to sleep.

The next morning when David woke up, he went in to see about his wife and found her dead in bed. He was charged with murder, and taken to court. All through the questioning he would say, "If I have done anything to her, if I had anything agin' her, I never knowed it," and he always said the same thing. He claimed his innocence to the very end.

However, the community got sort of riled up about it, she being a sweet young girl, and the killing got a lot of publicity. On purely circumstantial evidence, David was convicted of murder and was to be hanged on a tree just outside of town. When the time for the hanging came, there were people on both sides of Main Street in Cynthiana. They put him on a wagon, took him out to the tree, and hanged him.

When he was buried, the general tales kept going about what he had done. These were added to by various people trying to scare children and bring about obedience by telling about David Shelly's ghost. It was confirmed in various places that he was seen by a party of youngsters at a house. His bones were dug up, and a doctor kept them in hope that this would stop the hauntings, but it did not.

This ghost story has been carried down through the years in Harrison County. The court case is the most famous one in the county, and its records are in the courthouse where all the cases since 1792 are filed. This one box that has Shelly's trial in it is worn around the edges where people from all over the country have come to read the actual verdict and to write stories about it. There have been stories in magazines, newspapers, and books, all over the country, about the famous ghost of David Shelly who was supposed to have killed his wife.

Each year on the anniversary of his hanging, David appears to different people in Cynthiana. Perhaps this is because he was innocent. But the story has a happy ending, an ending that probably is the reason the story has been kept alive. One of the fishermen confessed on his deathbed that he was the one who had killed Mrs. Shelly. David Shelly's name was finally freed of the guilt that the community had put upon it.

*Female, age 50, Harrison County*

## Indian Ghost

Our leader was a forest service man and told us this story. It's centered on the Kentucky River, where there lived an Indian tribe. Since this was their hunting ground, they would always come in hunting parties. But one of the Indians was falsely accused of stealing another man's pelts that he had caught, with great effort, with his bow and arrows. They caught the Indian "thief," and as punishment, put him to death by stoning him. They were in the marshlands, so they threw his body in the marsh and didn't give him a decent burial.

This disgraced his family and children. Since he was killed at night and in the marshland, the fumes and marsh gases combined with his body and his soul, and his spirit absorbed some of the phosphorous in the water. To get revenge on this Indian tribe that had left his body unburied, his glowing spirit wandered around the marshland. Still to this day, if you go along the Kentucky River around midnight, you can see an Indian walking along the shoreline as a ghostly specter; you can see an outline in the night.

*Male, age unknown, Clark County*

## Great-Grandmother's Spirit

When I was thirteen, my great-grandmother died at my grandparents' house in the room where my brother and I slept when we visited. She was eighty-five.

A couple of months later, my brother and I went to my grandparents' to stay for a few days. All the way from our house to my grandparents', about thirty miles, I thought about staying in that room, and it bothered me. I dreaded it. I just knew that I was going to see her. Somehow I knew it. We went to bed in that room that night. During the night, I'd wake up and peek out into the room. Finally, I woke up and looked over at the wall opposite the bed, and I saw this misty shape sort of rounded on top and elongated.

I thought I wasn't really wide awake, but then I realized that I could clearly see the picture on the wall behind the shape! I got scared and ducked under the covers, and stayed awake a long time under there. I prayed not to be bothered by a ghost. I got hot under the covers and finally had to uncover my head, but I wouldn't open my eyes for anything!

I didn't see anything the next night or any time after that. I don't know if I psyched myself or not, but that image has stayed with me and it sure shook me.

*Male, age 46, Fayette County*

## Haunting at Old Fort Harrod

I was working at *The Legend of Daniel Boone* in Harrodsburg. There was a ghost in the theater that has been there for a very long time. It's where Fort Harrod is, so there are a lot of graves. The ghost has been seen on negatives of pictures before, and it has also been seen during Stripe Night. It was seen just leaning against a tree. It was a kind of blue form.

So one night, we were doing the show, and it was the first act. One of the guys who played the Indian felt a tap on his shoulder; he turned around and there was no one there. And he felt it again later on, when he was going to make an entrance, a tap on the shoulder. (This was on the left side of the stage.) Again he turned around and nobody was there. There was a girl in the production, Celeste, who was into witchcraft. The fellow went to her and said, "Something is going on," and he explained what was happening. She said she'd watch things to see what happened.

In the wedding scene, an actor named Chuck F. saw the ghost. There was a girl standing next to him, and she saw Chuck just staring and looking, but she couldn't see anything. He said it was a blue form, and he went and told Celeste. When intermission came, Anne, the girl who works in the box office, came backstage looking for Celeste. She felt like the ghost was speaking through her. She kept saying, "It starts with an A."

Anne was acting like she was on drugs; she talked slow, and was really disoriented. She felt that the ghost was there and calling her. I saw her and she didn't look like her regular self.

Then the second act came and there was this great big battle scene where torches were thrown over the wall. Everything went wrong. The Indians were throwing torches, and they were landing in the wrong places. It could have been because everyone was scared.

After the show was over, as we were leaving the theater, Anne said, "It's this way," and she started walking. Chuck grabbed her hand and she drug him along.

Celeste said, "Let everybody leave, then I want Anne and Roger and Chuck to come back and get rid of the ghost." We waited in the apartment until they got back to tell us what happened.

They went back to the theater that night. Celeste took a candle and walked around the region where the ghost lived. She sat the candle down midway in the area and walked on up the hill. She asked Roger to protect her by watching her and waking her up if she stopped breathing.

Anne and Chuck were out in the audience area watching. She asked to be protected and took the candle off the hillside and carried it away with her. Anne, Chuck, and Roger testified that they heard wagon wheels, and that they saw a dog run by. They said you could even hear his feet on the pavement.

Celeste said she met the being, and it was a young girl who was dressed up and her name was Anna. They left the theater, and everyone felt good about it except Anne. She still felt funny until they walked by the graveyard. Chuck was still holding her hand. As they got near the graveyard, Celeste and Roger turned around. Anne kinda waved good-bye to the graveyard and walked on past it, and she was alright after that.

*Female, age 25, Mercer County*

## Axe-Wielding Ghost

From one certain tomb a lady would come up and chase you with an axe right out of the graveyard. She also would throw things at you. I have never seen her, but they say it is true.

*Male, age 40, Scott County*

## Ghostly Appearance

Over at Elm Street by the railroad tracks, they said that there is an

Indian hut. There is an Indian girl who comes out in the moonlight. She only comes out, though, at a certain moonlight, and if you make a noise, she will go back in.

*Male, age 40, Scott County*

## Another Version of "Ghostly Appearance"

Well, you see, there's this cave outside of Georgetown. It's called the Indian Hut, and they call her the Indian Hut girl. You go in this cave, and that girl, the Indian Hut girl, lives there.

Every once in a while on a clear night (now it has to be a clear night) and a full moon, then that Indian woman will come out on the edge of a cliff, dressed in her Indian clothes.

She wears her Indian clothes, and if she hears you make a noise she will come out and chase you. But it has to be a really clear night and there has to be a full moon, you see.

*Male, age unknown, Scott County*

## Shadow of the Dead

This lady's husband killed himself in back of her grandmother's house. Every day at noontime, you can see the shadow of this dead man at the spot where he killed himself.

*Male, age 25, Scott County*

## Chief Pluggy's Ghost

In the early days, Captain Gano had to leave his wife to go get game for food. He would tell her not to go out and not to allow anyone in the cabin since the nearest neighbor was six miles away. Mrs. Gano promised to keep the house locked, but along about dusk, someone started pounding at the door. That someone was an Indian who said he knew the Captain.

This Indian was named Chief Pluggy Big Foot, and he kept pounding 'til Grandma Gano fired a gun through the door and killed him. Afterward the Ganos had no more trouble with Indians. It is said that Chief Pluggy Big Foot is buried by Big Branch, where you can still hear him moaning.

*Male, age unknown, Scott County*

## Lexington Church

The church is a big old spooky building and has an interesting history. The burial ground for the cholera epidemic is now under the foundation of the church. All of these graves were supposedly moved when the church was started, all except one grave. By the time the builders discovered they had missed one grave, it was too late to move it without tearing up the foundation of the church. The person who is buried under the church is John Bradford, the editor of Lexington's first newspaper. There is a small door leading underneath the sanctuary to the grave. But it is possible that some other remains were also missed.

———, the pastor's daughter, says they no longer pay much attention to the somewhat spooky things that occur in the church. Sometimes people will hear things in the building for which there is no explanation. One time ——— was in the church with her brother. She was on the phone, and she asked her brother not to leave her, but he did anyway. After she hung up the phone, she heard footsteps upstairs in the sanctuary. Thinking it was her brother, she called to him to come downstairs and stop trying to scare her. As she was calling to him, he walked in from the basement from an outside door. She told him about the footsteps. He checked the sanctuary, but there was nothing there!

One morning ———'s father went in the church, and a lady was standing there. He asked her how she had gotten in since all the doors were locked, and she simply said, "Through the door." She was disheveled and her hair was weird looking. She asked the Reverend for a dollar, promising to pay him back. He gave her the dollar, and she left. One morning a week later he unlocked the doors, went in, and found an envelope with a dollar in it lying in the middle of the floor. It had been raining, and there was a puddle of water near the money, but there were no wet footprints, and the outer doors were locked.

The church has a problem keeping janitors. They hear weird noises at night when they are shoveling coal. Then, when they learn about the grave under the sanctuary, they usually quit. When you are alone in the sanctuary, you can hear the chandeliers clinking, but there is no wind! One day the church secretary and the pastor heard a strange sound, like somebody walking wearing a plastic raincoat. They followed the sound, but it always stayed ahead of them. They never found its source.

Once, —— was practicing piano there by herself, and she heard a whistling at the front door. She got a little scared and decided to go out the back door. When she reached the back door, though, the whistling was there, right outside the door. She went to a side door, and the whistling was there, too. So she waited until the whistling sound went away, and then left quickly.

Before the present building was constructed in 1913, there had been two church buildings on the same site. They both burned. The present building was completed on a Christmas Eve. One day ——'s father had a premonition he could not shake, and, even though he lived in Georgetown, he felt strangely compelled to go check the church. Feeling somewhat sheepish about his premonition, he nearly turned back, but when he arrived, he found that one room was full of smoke. As it turned out, the furnace had overheated, and if he had not felt compelled to go check on the church, it would have burned down, just like its predecessors.

Haunted? I don't know, but I do know that, as —— says, "When you go in there, you just don't feel like you're alone."

*Female, age 21, Scott County*

*The church in the preceding story is First Baptist Church on West Main Street in Lexington. It seems the church was built on a site that used to be a burial ground. A few remnants of the old burial ground remained, including some from the cholera epidemic that swept through Lexington in 1833 and killed five hundred people.*

*The premonition at the end of the story may have been a coincidence, but it could also have been an example of a spirit nudging someone to take action in order to prevent a disaster.*

## This Ghost Will Chase You

It's out on North Hamilton Street [in Georgetown]. There's this graveyard, I forget the name of it. It has to happen at 12 midnight. There's this certain grave—I don't know which one—but at midnight you go to this grave. You holler across it, "Pabst Blue Ribbon," three times. You have to holler it across three times, now, over this certain grave. Then the woman in that grave comes out, and she will chase you with an axe.

*Male, age unknown, Scott County*

## Notes

1. Katherine Ramsland, *Ghosts: Investigating the Other Side* (New York: Thomas Dunne Books, 2001), 23–25.

*Chapter 2*

# Disappearing Ghosts

Disappearing ghosts make themselves known by manifesting in human form rather than by moving objects, creating disturbances, or making eerie sounds. Some of these ghosts are seen only in particular conditions or settings, probably associated with their earthly life, while others may be encountered at various places. The latter is true of the ghost in the first story in this chapter, "Walking Companion."

Sometimes ghosts seem to seek human contact. They may even walk along beside a person or sit in a car, and the mortal receives quite a shock when the ghost suddenly disappears. In a few cases ghosts may pursue the person for a short time, but they seem more likely to disappear suddenly.

It is apparent that not all spirits wish to be seen and so may disappear when they are sighted. The spirit that lives in a house may be as disturbed by an encounter as are the mortal inhabitants. This could be the case in "Confederate Soldier Returns," in this chapter.

The most common type of "disappearing ghost" story is that of the vanishing hitchhiker, a theme so popular that it was even used on an episode of *The Twilight Zone,* and as the title of a book by folklorist Jan Brunvand. In earlier days when fewer people had cars, hitchhikers were more prevalent and were routinely given rides, unlike today, when this is considered an unwise practice.[1]

These stories usually have something to do with a fatal accident that happened during travel, and they involve the ghost trying to complete the journey. (This type of ghost is, therefore, also dealing with unfinished business.) We are not always sure where the ghost is going, but it often seems willing to spend eternity trying to get there. This type of ghost raises some intriguing questions. Are the vanishing hitchhiker and its ilk conscious of their actions, and do they act with intent, or are they a form of trapped energy endlessly repeating an action but with no real awareness of self or of their effects on others?

Because the vanishing hitchhiker is so common, one familiar with ghost tales may groan when she realizes she is about to hear another version. But with careful listening, she may hear different circumstances than before, and new twists on the familiar theme. This chapter closes with several versions of this popular form.

## Walking Companion

My brother had a rare experience about sixty or seventy years ago. He was going to Lexington to school and was coming back on the Inter-urban at eleven o'clock at night. [The Inter-urban, a trolley line that ran from Georgetown to Lexington, was used by workers, students, and shoppers.] He would ride out to Lexington Pike from home on a horse and tie it there. Then he would go on the Inter-urban. When he came home, he'd come back on the Inter-urban, get on his horse, and ride home.

When he got off one night, nigh on 11:30, the horse was gone, so he had to walk home. He got about halfway home, and there was a place on the Pisgah Road about a hundred yards long where the trees on each side of the road hung clear over and made a canopy. It was dark as pitch in there. He had gotten almost through, when suddenly there was a woman walking right along beside him dressed in a black, black dress, and a black hat with a veil over her face, and everything. She was just there! She didn't say anything. She kept step with him. He kept stepping faster and faster, and she would keep stepping faster and faster. He finally broke into a run. He was about a mile and a half from home, and he came on home in a dead run.

That woman disappeared when he broke into a run—she just

disappeared. She's been appearing in Georgetown. She's made several appearances to people when they're walking home at night. This woman in black will be walking along beside them. They turn around and look at something. Then they look back and she's gone, no more signs of her at all. She was seen by I don't know how many people. Half the town was talking about her. This was the occurrence when my brother saw her out in the country.

Nobody knew who she was. She was always dressed the same, and she never said a word. She would just appear for about one-half minute or so and then disappear. Now that would scare anybody.

*Male, age 87, Woodford County*

## A Haint Can't Cross Water

I grew up in the northwest part of Bourbon County, and Silas Creek ran through for about one mile on my father's and grandfather's farms. Most of the laborers were black then, but most people who employed them called them Negroes or colored.

When I was about twelve years old, a favorite of mine was Uncle Aaron Brent, who was then around seventy years old. He was born a slave into the family of John Gano Hill, a Baptist preacher who was a chaplain in the Revolutionary War and who had baptized George Washington.

Uncle Aaron said that he was born with a veil over his eyes that allowed him to see the restless dead who stayed and traveled on the earth after death.

I remember well his tale of going over to Jacksonville one afternoon to see a farmer about cutting corn by the shock. The man was not at home and didn't get in until the moon was up and shining bright—an October harvest moon.

After seeing the farmer, Uncle Aaron got on his spring wagon pulled by old Max, his well-thought-of horse. About a mile out of Jacksonville, a man walking in the road asked Uncle Aaron for a ride. The man sat on the seat with him and talked of people and things in the neighborhood. After riding about a mile and a half, they came to Silas Creek. Uncle Aaron said the man vanished as they went over the water, for a haint can't cross water.

*Male, over 65 years, Bourbon County*

*Folklore maintains that people born with a veil or caul over their eyes can "see the restless dead," or things others cannot see. Persons with "the veil" often keep it to themselves.*

## Young Man with a Double Veil

Chuck can see things, 'cause Chuck was born with a double veil over his face. One time when we lived down on Eighth Street, when Chuck was young, Chuck and Pudd had been to the show and they were walking, coming up Fifth Street. And Chuck said he could see over by the Dunbar school, said he looked out thata way and saw a great big red ball of fire up in the sky.

And then, when we lived up on Black Rock, we'd be walking one night comin' from church, and Chuck saw somethin' and nobody saw it but Chuck. Chuck kept tryin' to show Pudd. We were walkin' along, we was hustlin' goin' along there, walkin', goin' home.

We used to walk around Black Rock all the time, got used to the idea of walkin' around Black Rock. He saw a man goin' through the tobacco field. (Nobody else could see it.) There used to be an old house right there at the corner of that old field. It must of burned down years ago, I guess after '37. (But mostly, folks are 'fraid to see what Chuck does.) Chuck would always see things when he was real little.

*Female, age 60, Carroll County*

## Vanishing Ghost

This is a story about a woman at Stamping Ground. Supposedly one night this woman in a white nightgown ran across the road in front of a car and disappeared. When the driver got out of his car to see if he had hit her, the woman had disappeared. Many nights afterward cars would line up in Stamping Ground to see if she would appear. Some nights later a woman did run across the road again, but it turned out she was a fake trying to keep the story going.

I do not believe in ghosts, but I do believe that the devil has bought the souls of some people. The Evil Prince has power, and you can become one of his workers. The Bible says this.

*Male, age 65, Scott County*

## Floating Apparition

Just this side of Stamping Ground, supposedly about five nights in a row, something floated across the road. It was never proven. People claim to have seen something, but they didn't know what it was. This happened in the summer of 1950.

*Male, age 30–40, Scott County*

## Cloudy Morning Apparition

Well, I've been living in Kentucky, in Scott County, for fifty-three years, and I was always told in Lexington around Leestown Pike that there was a lady killed over thataway. And so they said every Friday if it's a cloudy, rainy day, at one o'clock in the morning you can pass by, she'll be dressed in white, and she'll cross the road. If you stop to look back when she gets over to the cemetery by the road, she'll vanish. Several people have seen that and so, whether or not it's true, several people have told the story of that.

*Male, age 56, Scott County*

## Bed Corners Pulled

My mother's family supposedly lived in a haunted house when she was young. They never really heard of anything except on one night. My mother and her sisters were sleeping when Mom felt the covers being tugged from the bottom. She looked up and saw this black woman with a red bandanna on her head standing at the bottom of the bed. She nudged her sister to show her this lady. Micky woke up, but she didn't see the lady, although she did feel the covers being tugged. No one else had seen this lady before in the house.

*Female, approximately 35, Scott County*

## Confederate Soldier Returns

During my freshman year, my roommate was telling me some things that had happened in her house. She lived in Cynthiana. The house was built so that her parent's bedroom opened into the living room. It was an old house, and it was known to creak and groan.

One night her parents heard a strange noise in the living room, and they got up to see what it was. When they looked in at the door, they saw a man in uniform. It was an old uniform, like a Confederate uniform. He was just walking around the room like he lived there. The only thing was, they could see right through him! And, when they spoke to him, he disappeared.

*Female, age 21, Harrison County*

## Vanishing Rider

There was a man at Great Crossing. He and his people went to town and came back later that day. When they neared their house, there was a white horse standing in the gateway and a man dressed in white sittin' on this horse. When they went through the gateway, it disappeared. It just vanished. But he was sittin', and the horse was standin' right there in that gateway when they pulled in. And it just vanished.

*Female, approximately 30, Scott County*

## Disappearing Woman

Well, I was just a-sittin' in the front room a-starin' at nothin' when I saw this woman come from behind the old schoolhouse on the hill. She had this big ol' black coat on an' I didn't see much else. At first I didn't pay no never-mind about her, but then she come down the lane and across the foot log. Well, I sat there watchin' her, then I says to myself, "What would a woman be doin' a-comin' this way?"

Well, I got up and went to the kitchen to look out the winder at her to see who she was. I took one look, then I looked again, and she disappeared into thin air. The dogs weren't barkin', and they always bark when somebody comes by. The chickens weren't squawkin' either, so I don't know what it was I saw. Mebbe it was some dead relation, I don't know. I never did catch a look at her again.

*Male, approximately 65, Boyle County*

## Field Hand's Struggle

I had for about twenty years a white man, Will J., who worked for me and lived in a house on the farm. He, I believe, is still living at Lair Station in Harrison County. Will said that one time when he was about eight years of age, he took a job of housing tobacco on the Sam Houston farm, on the road that connects Paris and Jacksonville. Mr. Houston, when night come, told one of his tenants to take Will home for supper and bed. The home is a very large, old, frame house, two stories tall, large rooms, and in the attic there were several smaller rooms. One of these was given to Will. In the night, being rather chilly, he put a blanket over the top sheet. Twice during the night he awoke and found all the covers on the floor. He said he thought that some of the other hands were playing a trick on him. However, the next night, he decided to move a dresser in front of the door and check the windows.

After being asleep for a couple of hours, Will woke up cold and discovered all the top bedclothes on the floor. He placed the covers up on the bed again and decided to stay awake and learn what was going on. All at once, the covers were moving to the foot of the bed and slipped through his grasp.

Will said that he didn't stay there anymore, and he found out that a man had been murdered about seventy-five years before in that attic by having his throat cut.

*Male, age 65–70, Scott County*

## Fellow Traveler

There was a man murdered at Turkey Foot. They buried him in the Hinton Graveyard at Turkey Foot. He came back, and when anyone would go down the road at night, he would walk with them—walk right along beside them. Or if they were on a horse, he would get on the back of the horse. Soon as he got to the edge of the cemetery, he would disappear. He did it with everybody that passed that cemetery at night.

*Female, age unknown, Scott County*

## The Possessed Pontiac

My father bought this older Pontiac that had belonged to an old lady who had recently died. Her husband had bought it for her before he died, and it was very special to her, according to her relatives that sold him the car.

She took care of the car, and even though it was over ten years old, it looked new. My father used it to drive to work, and he commented on feeling strange, like there was someone in the car with him, so he kept it locked. He also said there was an odor of face powder he couldn't get rid of.

He was driving home one night. It was storming and raining. He wasn't going too fast, but it was very hard to see, and suddenly the brakes went on, and the car slid to a stop. But he didn't have his foot on the brake!

It threw him forward, and he was sitting back in his seat when he looked over at the passenger side. He saw the face of a white-haired older woman, and he said she smiled at him and disappeared!

Well, he was shook, and, rain or no rain, he got out of the car. That's when he discovered that he had stopped just ten feet from a flooded bridge, and the water was just rushing across it!

*Female, age 20, Fayette County*

## Little Boy in the Strawberry Patch

My baby brother, Danny, was two years old, and every morning, he'd go to our neighbor's garden and eat strawberries. He'd sit in the middle of the garden and eat strawberries. When he got up in the morning, the first thing he'd do was go to that garden.

When our neighbors were away, he drowned. They didn't know that because they were on a trip. When they got back from their trip about two weeks after he drowned, they called on the telephone. My mother answered, and they said, "Mrs. W., Danny's in our garden, and he's eating our strawberries."

Well, my mother just went crazy, and had a nervous breakdown. My daddy got on the telephone, and he said, "Who is this?" Then he told them, "Look, Danny drowned two weeks ago!"

The neighbors got very upset. When they turned back to look at the garden, to see if he was still sitting there, he was gone.

*Female, age 35, Henry County*

## Hitchhiker Ghost

This is the story of the vanishing woman. This story took place in a little town, five miles north of Georgetown, called Great Crossing. Rumor has it that a certain woman was on her way to visit her mother in the hospital in Georgetown. She was driving a little fast, had an accident, and was killed. On certain nights of the year, people said they picked up a young lady. She wanted a ride to Georgetown to the hospital. They talked to her normally until they reached the hospital. Then they looked over when they reached their destination, and no one was there.

*Interviewer: Is this still going on?*

Yes, on certain nights of the year, driving through Great Crossing by yourself, you might look around and someone would be sitting in your car with you.

*Male, age 40, Scott County*

## Taxi Rider

There was this young girl standing near a cemetery. She was standing beside the road and flagged down a taxi driver. She told him her name and where to take her.

When they got to the house where she wished to be dropped off, she told him to go inside and they would pay him. She got out of the car and started walking. He went into the house to get his money. The taxi driver told them the girl's name and told them she said they would pay for her ride. This girl was their daughter who had been dead five years.

*Male, approximately 40, Scott County*

## Vanishing Hitchhiker

This couple was going to the prom, and they had a wreck. The guy was killed, and the girl was going for help when she was killed by a car. Every year on a certain date, people will see a young girl in a white gown, walking along that spot, crying. They will pick her up, and when she gets in the car, she'll just vanish.

*Female, age 18, Madison County*

## Notes

1. Jan Harold Brunvand, *The Vanishing Hitchhiker* (New York: W. W. Norton, 1981).

# Chapter 3

# Mysterious Events and Haunted Places

According to one so-called expert, "Ghosts live in vacant houses, eat 'ghost toasties,' and drink evaporated milk!" Some places, vacant or not, are associated with mysterious events or hauntings. The mysterious or haunted place may be an abandoned house or a specific part of an occupied house, or it may be a natural area like a woods or a cave.

The story "Mysterious Circle" in this chapter was told by a Central Kentucky resident who knew of a haunted area in North Carolina. People in the area call it the "Devil's Stamping Ground," and it is a clear circle in the woods where nothing grows.[1]

It may seem that newer houses would be free from hauntings, since these buildings haven't been around long enough to acquire ghosts. Nevertheless, a number of stories have been recorded of supernatural happenings in contemporary homes. This chapter contains such stories. These hauntings are less often reported, probably because the residents feel they will be ridiculed for claiming that their house has a ghost, or because they fear such knowledge could negatively affect the value of their property.

Similarly, employers often refuse requests to interview employees about a reputed ghost or poltergeist in their place of business or to have their property photographed because of its ghostly association. Most mortals do not want to be associated with death in any way, and perhaps employers feel this sort of attention would negatively affect the public attitude toward their enterprise.

Some of the stories in this section do not involve a ghost at all, but instead explore the death lore and superstitions surrounding human corpses, as in the story "Experience Transporting a Corpse." The story was told in a way that was supposed to be humorous, but the event was not funny to the storyteller's partner at the time. Humorous ghost stories can serve the purpose of lessening the fear of death for some tellers and hearers (but not for others).

## Traveling House

There's this house in Oxford, on the Cynthiana Pike, where some people were killed. Some fellow came through there real late at night, and he noticed this house that sat right at the edge of the road, because it was so close, you see.

When he came back through there another time, he looked for this house, but he couldn't find it. He couldn't find one close to the road, so he went up to another house, and knocked on the door, and asked 'em if there wasn't a house upside of the road.

They said it must be that house over there. He said it looked like it, but it was settin' up on a rise, back from the road.

They told him it was that house all right, that it traveled at night sometimes. They said lots of people'd seen it down by the road late at night. They said some fellers got killed there when it used to set close to the road 'fore it got moved some time back.

*Male, age 40, Scott County*

## The Three-Dimensional Shadow

My best friend in high school, he lived in a house out in the country near the interstate. And he said that, when he lived there, when he was a kid, that there was this dark shape that moved around the house sometimes. You know, it was just like a shadow, only it wasn't just a flat shadow against the wall. It was like a shadow that comes out into the room, you know.

*Interviewer: 3-D?*

A three-dimensional shadow, yeah, and he said that, like, a lot of times he would go to bed at night, and he would look around, and that thing would be standing about four feet from him. And then it would just . . . you could see it moving around.

He said his grandfather lived there a lot longer than he had. It would get a lot closer to his grandfather than it would to him. His grandfather, once or twice, he would put his hand through it and nothing happened. His hand just went through it.

Nobody in the family was scared of it or anything; it never did anything. He grew up with it, so he thought nothing of it. His grandfather thought nothing of it, 'cause he'd lived a long time in that house. I think that somebody got killed there, in the house . . . but it was a friendly ghost.

*Female, age 20, Scott County*

## Walking Ghosts

At the corner of Oxford Road and Muddy Ford there's a house. And there was a man killed on the back porch. A family moved in there and said they couldn't sleep at night 'cause somebody was always walking around out there. They finally moved.

*Female, age unknown, Scott County*

## The Hanging Tree

This story is about a deserter of the Civil War. Unfortunately, I'm not sure whether he was a Confederate or a Union soldier. They hung him from a tree that stands in front of a house in Owen County. It's on the Caney Creek Road. For many years, his boots were left hanging in the tree to be a reminder to other deserters of the war, and now sometimes people see his ghost there.

*Female, age unknown, Owen County*

## Redheaded Ghost

Aunt Bea said she saw some redheaded woman lookin' in the window one night. She was looking in the window and was dying laughing. The redheaded woman used to come to the house all the time.

Once, as Bea and Deak were sleeping one summer night, it was hot, and she was in one bed and Deak was in another. Seemed like the redheaded woman came through the room and pulled all the covers off of her. She said she jumped up, jumped out of her bed, and ran in there and got in bed with Deak.

*Female, age unknown, Carroll County*

## Headless Ghost

We used to hear these stories about a ghost, close to my house on the road to Murpheysville. The road goes through these woods. It curves around, and it goes up this big hill, and there's a house up on top of the hill. Supposedly, back in the old days, there used to be this headless guy who would hop on the back of carriages, ride to the top of the hill, and hop off.

*Male, age 40, Bourbon County*

## Suicide's Bloodstain

This story was about the "old Paine farm." It is said that a girl had killed herself in the house about eighty years ago. They say where she died there were huge bloodstains, and on the anniversary of her death the bloodstains become more vivid and richer. That's the only time that the bloodstains are vividly seen.

*Female, age 30–40, Scott County*

## The House of Dreams

*The following are accounts of the experiences of a husband and wife.*

*Wife's account:* It started out that we went out to look at this trailer. That night I had a dream that we lived in this old house on this farm and that I had a car wreck. I was four months pregnant, and I dreamed I was hemorrhaging. Blood was just pouring from my waist down. The next day I almost had a miscarriage. I was bleeding, and I had to go to the hospital.

Three weeks later, this guy came and asked us about movin'

onto his farm. So we went ahead and moved. We didn't know that the farm I dreamed about was next door to the place we moved. It was on the same farm, just on a different place on the farm. This older guy, who had lived in the old house I had the dream about, came over, and I told him that I had a dream about the house.

He laughed and said, "What did you dream about?" I said that there were no closets in the house, and that upstairs there was an old wardrobe full of clothes. There were witches and warlocks in the room, tryin' the clothes on. I walked up into the room and they started squeezin' me around the waist, and at this time I was six months pregnant in my dream (but I was really just four months pregnant at the time).

Then, when I really was six months pregnant, my sister-in-law, who I was really close to, was in a car wreck. She was hit in the stomach, and blood was pouring from her. She was paralyzed from the waist down, and she died in the car wreck.

It was just this house; you had to feel it to really know. I called it a evil house. This guy who had lived there said if I'd lived a hundred years ago, they'd have burned me at the stake for having premonitions like that.

*Husband's account:* My wife dreams about things. She dreamed she was bleeding and paralyzed. She dreamed about the house on the farm where we lived and I worked. It was used by warlocks upstairs in her dream and was terrifying. It didn't have any closets, but there was a chest sitting in a room in her dream.

When my wife was dreaming about the house and that she was paralyzed and bleeding from the waist down, on July 7, my brother got killed in a motorcycle accident. He was destroyed from the waist down. Three days later in the same area, my sister-in-law was in a car wreck, and she was destroyed from the waist down.

She told me about the dream she was havin' before these wrecks. I was workin' the farm, so I went in this old house, upstairs and around the house. This house is a really old house, and it still has the chains where they chained slaves in the basement and in a building out back so they wouldn't run away.

But in the house upstairs, it was really spooky. When I went upstairs, I couldn't believe I was seeing what I was seeing. She had described the wardrobe, the stairways, the lack of closets, and everything in the room upstairs, where the warlocks were supposed to be, just as it was.

I went in there and the clothes in the old wardrobe were there, and I just couldn't believe my eyes. It was unbelievable. From then on, I was scared of the house. I had to work the farm, but I wouldn't go around that house. I stayed as far away from it as I could. In the few times I went around, I would think that I saw someone standing in the window. So I would vary my path to get further away from it.

But before long, in a month's time, I found myself working up to the house, and then I was going in the house and remodeling it. I was no longer scared of the house, and I was growing quite fond of it. When I finally broke away from it, it was amazing how scary all that was. It had almost got me!

Ten years before we lived on the farm, there was another family lived there. Their little boy, on his way to catch the school bus, passed by this big house. He was run over and killed in the driveway. That house has really got a history.

*Female, age 35, and male, age 35, Henry County*

## "Nothing to Worry About"

When I was a boy, about four years old, I got out of bed early in the morning. I walked into the living room, and the rocking chair was rocking by itself.

I stood there watching just a moment when my grandmother came into the room from her bedroom. I remember that she had on her pink housecoat. She walked straight over to the chair and put her hand on the back and stopped it. She looked at me and said, "It's just the wind."

Well, I didn't say yea or nay, but I didn't feel any wind. There were no outside doors or windows open anyway.

That wasn't the last time that the rocking chair rocked by itself, either. My grandmother would just tell me it was nothing to worry about.

*Male, age 46, Scott County*

## The Mysterious Circle

The Devil's Circle is near Greensboro, North Carolina. It's in books—I read it in a book. And there's a picture of it; it's just a big brown hole like a circle. It's not really a hole, it's just a circle, and nothing grows in it; it's just dusty. It's in a wooded area.

My brother lives in Greensboro, and he goes to college up there. Some of his friends have been to it. They went one night (not my brother, but some of his friends) and slept in it, and the next morning when they woke up, they were off in the woods a few feet away from it.

*Interviewer: What's the story behind the circle?*

Nobody knows what caused it, and nobody knows anything about it really, as far as I can tell. My brother told me that he had heard that people had sat in there, and stayed up all night, and they never said another word afterward, but I don't know if I believe that or not. They were, you know, just mute or something, whatever you call it. They said they were probably scared to death about something, just so scared that they could not talk again. I told my brother I'd send scientists down there, put plants in it to see if they'd die; I think they would.

*Male, age 20, Scott County*

## Dove Spirit

These men were digging up a coffin to move it someplace else. They got to talking, and one of them said, "I wonder what a dead man looks like after he's been dead a long time."

Well, some wanted to see, but some didn't think that it was the thing to do. The ones who wanted to see inside the coffin decided they'd open it anyway.

So they started taking an axe to it. The other fellows didn't like it, and they said so, but these men hacked away at it anyway.

They'd took a couple of hacks when, out of nowhere, a white dove landed on top of the coffin. They backed off fast then, and left the coffin undisturbed.

*Male, age 50, Grant County*

## Young Ghost Hunters

I heard this one from a fraternity brother. He lives in Baltimore, and when he was thirteen or fourteen, there was this baseball field real close to where he lived. Some four-foot-high grasses ran along it, and a fringe and a wooded area were back behind it.

He said that there was a tale that a guy shot himself out there close to where he lived. He and some friends of his decided to go out there one time and see what the story was. They went out into this wooded area, and they heard something. It scared 'em so they took off running across this baseball field. Then all of a sudden they turned around. My friend turned around first, and he said he saw this man sitting in a chair backward, just sitting there looking at 'em.

He said they all turned around and looked at him, stood there for a couple of seconds, ya know, just looking at him, really scared. Then they ran away. I think he said he can describe him, what he looked like and everything.

*Interviewer: It's supposed to be the guy that killed himself?*

I think so. But it was nobody that he knew and he lived right around there. It was nobody that any of the rest of the kids knew either, and there were about four or five of 'em. He was just suddenly sitting there in a chair, ya know, right at the edge of the baseball field.

*Male, age 20, Scott County*

## Experience Transporting a Corpse

While I was working for a funeral home, I used to transport corpses when I was on duty. One night we got a call from Lexington to bring a corpse to Georgetown, so this other guy and I took the hearse to Lexington.

On the way back, the air escaped from the lungs of the corpse, and it sat up. It was covered up with a sheet and must have looked pretty spooky. I had seen this happen before, but the other guy was new.

When the corpse sat up, covered with a sheet, this guy just about—! He started yelling, and clawing at the door, and he managed to get it open!

So there I was, trying to drive the hearse, and holding on to this guy. I was all over U.S. 25, but I finally got it stopped. He finally settled down, and we drove on into Georgetown. But the next day he quit.

*Male, age 21, Scott County*

## Doesn't Believe in Ghosts?

About thirty years ago, I was teaching in rural Kentucky, where I was principal of a small consolidated high school. Teaching with me was a Centre College football player, a large, rough kind of person. One night, the weather was kind of like it is here today, cold and snowy. We were walking down the road, and we passed by a cemetery. This big football player said to me, "I don't believe in ghosts, but I'm mortally afraid of them." This was very funny to me because he was very large, and it seemed to me that he would be willing to face anything. He repeated, "I'm mortally afraid of them, although I don't believe in them."

*Male, age 65, Scott County*

## Light Pursues Car

My uncle told us about a time he was coming back from Frankfort on U.S. 62. He said he was just riding down the road, and, all of a sudden, he saw this big, bright light. He said it kept getting bigger and brighter, and it was following him down the highway.

The faster he went, the faster the light went. Then he put the gas all the way down. He said when he got about two miles from town, the light disappeared. He did not know what it was and did not care. He has not seen it anymore.

*Male, age 45, Scott County*

## Interfering Ghost

There was a two-part, two-story log house in back of the place. It had what we called a dog trot in between the parts. Also overhead, it was all solid.

They had some colored people that lived on this farm; they were tenant farmers. They ran out of room in the barn to put all of the loose hay, and these colored folks said, "Well, we're gonna take it and pitch it in the upper part of this old log structure there."

The owner said, "It won't be any use," and no one ever realized what he was talkin' about until a week later. They put this hay in there during the day and went back over there a week or so later and all the hay was laying back out on the ground. Nobody could keep hay up there, and nobody could ever explain it.

*Male, approximately 50, Harrison County*

## Candles in the Oratory

At one time some millionaire gave to the Jesuits a house, and they made of it a novitiate for young boys to study. Well, they found one room there that was strange.

There was a Father —— who was interested in these things, and one day he called my brother and said, "Paul, come upstairs. I have something to show you." And so he went up that night. There was an oratory where the young scholastics go to pray, and on the mantel there were two candles. Father —— lit these candles, and by the time he got to the door, they were out.

Well, Paul was in wonderment, you know, and Father —— said, "Now you go do it." Paul asked Father ——, "Do you have someone blowing back there?"

He said, "No, you go light them," and my brother went. He lit the candles, and by the time he got back to the door, they were out.

Now Father —— said they should go to another oratory, and they did. They lit candles, and they stayed lit. They were never able to find out why these candles, burnt in honor of some saint or the Lord, wouldn't burn in that room. They never did, and it was never solved.

*Female, age 60, Scott County*

# Clock That Refused to Run

I work on clocks, and I was called to this lady's house out on U.S. 25. I had started working on three or four clocks of hers. First she told me she had a grandfather clock no one could repair. She said, "We've had several people try."

I said, "Well, I'll be glad to look at it." So I went out and started working on her clocks. I worked on the grandfather and got it started, and I did quite a bit of work there in the house. I brought two clocks back home.

Well, that night about 11:30 or 12:00, the clock stopped 'cause they just left it without winding it. So I took one of the clocks back with me to put in the other clock's place until about three or four days later. I couldn't find a thing wrong with it. There was nothing wrong when I checked it over. I started it back up again and it ran, so I returned the clock to its owner.

I came back home, and it must have been forever since I'd called the lady. So I called and asked her how the clock was doing. She said, "Well, the hands have fallen off, and the clock has stopped."

So I went back out. I couldn't determine why the hands had fallen off, and I said, "This clock is a mystery."

And she said, "I knew that. Let me tell you a story about the clock. One reason why no one has been able to fix the clock is my husband's grandmother lived in a house right near here, and his father and mother married and lived in that house too, before they divorced. After the divorce, his mother said that no one would ever be happy in that house, and she would see to it, and this was her clock that was over in that house."

So the lady told me she wasn't happy. There was quite a bit of sadness there in the family and a lot of problems. She said at night that they'll go downstairs and there will be dishes just broken for no reason and they'll hear sounds, and chains clattering. And this is not a lady who is nuts. She said that her boys had heard the same sounds.

So I went ahead and worked on the clock while I listened to everything she said. Then I said maybe the house some way is sitting on a shelf, maybe there is some vibration. I said, "I'll just bolt the clock to the wall." And I took a huge bolt and bolted it to the wall, a toggle bolt, so it could never be moved. I started the clock back up.

I called her a while later, and she said, "Well, the clock has stopped again. I can't get inside to start it. Did you lock the door?"

"Well," I said, "no, ma'am. I don't have a key to the bottom of the clock." I had to see this. So I got out there and, sure enough, it's locked. I just couldn't believe it. Still really don't. So I made a key and unlocked the clock, and on the inside of the door was the key to the clock. It was hanging on the inside of the clock that had been locked up!

I said, "Now this clock is going to run if I have to keep coming out here from now on. It's going to run. I intend for it to run!" And, as far as I know, the clock still runs.

*Male, age 55, Scott County*

# Notes

1. Liv, "Haunted NC: Devil's Tramping Ground," Greensboring.com, http://greensboring.com/viewtopic.php?=10&t=993 (accessed December 17, 2008).

*Chapter 4*

# Presences Sensed by Light, Cold, or Sound

Popular themes of ghost stories are the feeling of cold spots and the hearing of strange noises that cannot be explained. Many stories, like death lore, involve the seeing of shadows and light. By nature, we want to explain all occurrences. The unexplainable causes great discomfort, which may be interpreted as fright. An inexplicable noise or sound conjures up images of ghosts for some people. Similarly, when a chill or a cold breeze is felt in the midst of warmth, some may think a dead person has returned.

Why do we assume a ghost is cold or creates a cold aura? Maybe we associate cold with death because, as warm-blooded creatures, we know that when the life force leaves us, our bodies become cold. Or maybe we think of the chill of the underground: graves are dug deep into the earth, where it is cooler than on the surface. Likewise, caves have been at least partially associated with death since our earliest ancestors stepped foot into them. Nighttime is also associated with death and ghosts. We have all experienced the fear of dark, chilly nighttime, when the sun, which warms us and provides us with the relative safety of its light, is not present.

The phenomena mentioned in these stories, light, cold, and sound, are the main criteria that are studied by ghost investigators as they attempt to prove or disprove supernatural events. Modern technology has made available devices that can monitor the unexplainable happenings in a particular place. Such devices include cameras that can sense the slightest change in light and shadow, monitors that can detect the most minute fluctuations in temperature, and very sensitive sound recorders that detect sounds at all decibel levels. These can be controlled by a computer program to run over a long period of time without a human (which might affect a spirit's actions) being present.[1]

The following stories reflect the above-mentioned themes: unexplained sounds, temperature changes, odors, and lights and spots that appear out of nowhere.

## Freezing Manifestations

This house is over a hundred years old. A girl lives there by herself because it is a family home, her father's home. The house has been in the family ever since her grandfather's time. It's a big colonial home with big white pillars and three floors.

The girl is a friend of mine. She has a cat, and she has told me that this cat would wake her at night hissing. You know how cats do. And every hair on the cat's back would be standing up, and he is pacing around the room. The cat would just be pacing, walking around the room growling and hissing, and she said the room would be freezing. This is the truth. She is not a dummy; she doesn't just believe in stuff like this at all.

The temperature drops and it scares her to death, but she won't tell her family because she doesn't want them to worry. So she picks the cat up and throws it out the bedroom door. She calls it "the cat spells." When the cat calms down, she lets him back in.

She just blames it on the cat. She really thinks there's something else but doesn't really know what it is. She has gotten so scared before that she has grabbed her purse and run out of the house at 3:30 in the morning and gone to her sister's house. She just gets a weird feeling because the temperature in the house drops, the whole house just freezes, and the cat goes crazy.

One time she came home and the television was on, and she hadn't turned it on for days. Also she's got a centerpiece with dried flowers and a bow. She always puts it up on an extremely high shelf— you know how you put things in special places—so the cat won't get into it because he would ruin the flowers. She has come in several times and the centerpiece is on the table and the flowers crushed.

Her brother was there one night last summer. He had just dozed off on the couch downstairs. He had been asleep for about ten minutes. It was about one o'clock in the morning, and he was dreaming. Have you ever waked yourself up talking? That's what happened. He was dreaming, and he heard someone say to him, "Mike, don't you think it's freezing in here?"

He said, "No, it's not cold in here. It's summer outside." Then he realized that someone had been talking to him, and he said the voice was really deep, a real deep but friendly voice. It wasn't a voice that would scare you, but he said it scared him to death anyway.

He lay there for a minute trying to decide what to do. He decided to trick the voice, so he kept his eyes closed. He realized now that he had *not* been dreaming. Someone had actually said the words to him. So he was lying there, and he said, "You know, it is cold in here. I'll go out and get wood for the fire." Now that's a dumb thing to say, but he was playing along with this thing.

He got up, and it *was* cold in that room. He could see his breath, no lie! He ran up to his sister's room and woke her up. She wouldn't go down. She said she knew how cold it gets and didn't want to experience this weird coldness and feeling if she didn't have to. They both slept upstairs the rest of the night.

I know this sounds ridiculous. I swear he says, "I cried when it happened," and when he told me about it, his eyes watered. It scares him just to think about it. I think this coldness comes when there is the presence of a dead person in the room . . . This is what scares me.

*Female, age 22, Fayette County*

## Cassius Clay's Wife Reappears

About three years before I was born, my father, who was a doctor, had bought this property which my mother found at Clays Ferry, Kentucky. It was on the Madison County side, and it had twenty-one acres of waterfront. At one time, a part of the house was a riverfront tavern. Cassius Clay had once owned this place. At the time when we bought the place, the part out front was not grass but rather a roadway that came straight up to the door. Later we put in a flag-stone walk.

Anyway, my oldest brother, Alfred, who was about fifteen at the time, had been ill, and we were staying at our place on the river. Daddy would come down on weekends. Alfred hadn't been well, so he was in this room over here [informant points to the front room on the first floor] and he was lying down by the window that was on the river side, looking into this room. [Informant points toward the stairway.]

Alfred happened to glance up, and he saw this woman walking by the door, and he watched her for a few minutes. He thought that was odd, because Maggie, the colored woman, was in the kitchen, and they were the only two people in the house. She was no one that he had ever seen before. She was that clear and plain, so later he said something to Mother about it, and she said, "Oh boy, I thought your temperature had gone down."

Mother said to describe the woman, and Alfred said she had not exactly red hair, but kind of reddish brown with a bun in the back, and he said she had on a funny dress that came up real high and which was on the brownish side. He said that she just walked past the door, and he thought she was just someone visiting and won-dered why she was dressed like that. He saw her two or three times.

Time went by. One night Alfred was sleeping upstairs, and he woke Mother up and said, "I heard a carriage running over brick." Well, Mother told him that he couldn't have heard a carriage running over brick because there was no brick around. It was all stone. But Alfred said, "I tell you I heard carriage wheels running over brick." He said he heard that two or three times. Well, when we decided to put in the stone walk, we had to dig down so far in order to lay the flagstone because they are so large in size. They were hand-dressed stone. They dug down, and all of a sudden they hit something: *brick,* herringbone weave, and it extended out the whole driveway!

Quite a bit of time went by. Alfred was attending Columbia University, and he was doing his thesis for his degree in Greek revival architecture, so of course he got quite interested in the types of architecture all over the state. I went with him quite a bit. He got interested in our house and also in White Hall, which is Cassius Clay's home. There was a great niece at White Hall, and we had to get permission from her to visit, because at that time it still belonged to the family. We went there. He did all of the measurements, outside pictures, inside pictures, and then he went to see the great niece.

She had a portrait in the living room. Alfred asked who the lady in the portrait was. She said she was Cassius Clay's very, very young wife. Here was the woman Alfred had seen years before, and she was dressed exactly the way he had described her years before!

They tell a story, and I don't know if it is true or not historically. I do know that Cassius Clay was ambassador to Russia, and he certainly did sire a son by one of the ladies of the Russian court. They said that the nursemaid was sent to the U.S. with his son, and they brought the child in a closed carriage to this house rather than to White Hall. Whether that is true or not, I don't know. It's just legend or lore.

*Female, age unknown, Madison County*

*Cassius Clay (1810–1903) was an eccentric, controversial figure in Kentucky history. He was an abolitionist and at one time an ambassador to Russia. His home, White Hall, in Madison County, Kentucky, is now owned by the state and is open to the public. Ghost sightings have been reported at White Hall, although none are included in this collection.*

## Party Ghost

Well, when I was about sixteen or so, a lot of my friends and I would go over to this one guy's house. His name was Billy. Billy's parents were loaded, and they didn't want to be bothered with his friends, so they built him a party house out in back of the big house. That way his parents wouldn't be bothered with the noise or anything.

Well, one night about ten or so of us were partying. It was about seven o'clock during the summer, so it was still pretty light. Anyway, there wasn't a bathroom in the party house. I had to go to the bathroom, so I went to the big house. His parents weren't home.

I was sitting there in the bathroom, and I heard the front door open and close and somebody walk up the stairs. I thought it was Billy, so I didn't get scared. I finished and went out to the hall where you could look up into the bedrooms upstairs. The stairs were right there. The bedrooms were in a kind of square, built around the stair steps. Anyway, I called for Billy, and he didn't answer. Well, I was on my way out the front door, and I heard a door slam. Then I heard the same footsteps coming down the upstairs hall. Well, let me tell you, I was scared to death. The strange thing was that I couldn't move or even scream. That was the first time in my life I couldn't say a word.

These footsteps came down the stairs. I swear I heard them but couldn't see a damn thing. Anyway, the steps walked right past me, and I could feel a slight breeze when they went past. They went out the front door, and then I heard horses. Billy didn't have any horses on the farm. Finally I got myself pulled together enough to run, and I took off toward the party house. When I got down there, Billy said I looked white as a ghost. I told him what had happened, and he freaked. He told me that the whole family had heard those footsteps and horses before. He said there was something strange around the house.

He told me that about three times he'd been driving home late, from a date or something, and he'd seen a noose, like someone was going to be hung, hanging from a tree in the long driveway to the house. We came to find out there had been a lynching on the property long ago. They never did find out what made those footstep sounds. But let me tell you what: I didn't go to the big house alone again.

*Female, age 25, Fayette County*

## Murdered Woman Returns

Before my grandmother died, she'd tell me stories about the house that my mother was born in. There was a woman lived there; her husband was crazy and chopped off her head, and he went to the pen. This is no legend. This is the truth.

My mother said when she was a little girl, they had bloodstains on the floor below the rugs. She said they could put Comet and everything—put lye on it and scrape it off—and she'd swear the next day the stains would be there again.

She said when she was a little girl, she and her mother would stay there alone. 'Course Grandpa and the boys would go to church, and, you know, back then they had to drive horses.

She said they'd be rocking in the rocking chair, her and my grandmother, by the fireplace at night, you know, listening to the radio. On the porch they'd hear footsteps of heavy feet and someone turning the doorknob, and the door would come unlatched.

She said one night Grandma and her were out on the porch rocking, about twilight. She said they saw a woman running down the road with a white gown on and a halo over her face, but you couldn't see her face, just her head.

*Male, age unknown, Bourbon County*

## Spirit Comes and Goes

Something keeps drawing me to this place. Upstairs I can hear noises walking across—seems like it goes more this way and then you'll hear them walking back for a while. You can hear somebody come down the stairs. You'll hear them go up the stairs. You'll hear the door open and then close, but you don't see nobody. You'll hear a car door open outside and the door slam, but you don't see no car, and there's no car out there. I've set here a lot of times and heard that.

I used to have a lock on that door where when you shut it, you had to lock it, turn the key in, to get it to stay locked. It wouldn't fasten no other way. I've got up and took the key out of the door and put it in my pocket. I'd say, "I don't know who you are, playing games with me, or what's going on, but you'll have to have a key to get out that door." That door would still open and close with me sitting here with the key in my pocket.

You can hear this walking up there a lot. I was sitting right here when my sons was gone. They said, "Ah, you're imagining things."

I know when I hear something and when I don't. I'm ignorant, but I ain't no fool.

I'm sitting in a chair, a car door slammed outside, front door opened, and they went upstairs. I'm saying, I didn't see nobody go up them stairs.

I gets up and I goes to the banister. I say, "Waynie, are you upstairs?" Nobody answers, and I'm starting walking up them stairs. Next thing I know, I'm up at the top of them stairs. I says, "Waynie, don't play games with me. Tell me if you're in here." I didn't hear nobody, didn't see nobody. I looked under the bed, looked in the closet—they's so full it's impossible to hide in there. I stopped, and thought, "Am I imagining this?"

I came down the stairs. I says, "Waynie, if it's you, let me know you're here." I looked in the bathroom and everything. The walking came from over here, across here, and stopped in the hallway up there.

Well, I've never bothered nobody in this house, never hurt nobody, never done nothing to nobody, but I wish whoever it was would let me know who it is anyway. . . . Well, I hear the walking again. I was sitting here and was looking up at the stairway when all of a sudden . . . whoo! . . . like it come right past me. I know it's happened in the kitchen. I thought, "What is going on here?" I go in the kitchen and listen in there, and there's, like, something fell in that closet in there, and there wasn't a thing out of place. I didn't say nothing else about it.

Daddy sitting where he's sitting (back bedroom next to the kitchen), he can hear noises, like a big crash or something. He was looking for it, I was looking for it, and my son Wayne was looking for it.

It goes inside, and it's like this *someone* is looking at me. I turn my head, and I can see her eyes, her face, and it just goes away. Mommy lays in that bed. She kept seeing this—looked like a man—looked out the door at her. She says, "D., come here and see if you don't see somebody."

I looked, but I didn't see nobody. She'd say, "You come here and just sit down here and see if you don't see him, too." That went on half the night. I went in and turned the shade light on, and the light has been on ever since. She says she don't see him when the light is on.

Right where he is setting, there were two places that came up in the middle of the floor, real bright, about that long [informant measures with her hands]—prettiest silver you ever looked at. Looking at it, it started fading away, and then it came right back up. Mommy was looking at it. Daddy and my son walked up and was standing there looking at it. I run in there and got a pan and a brush and was scrubbing it. I run my fingers through it, and it was real slick. I thought, "I got it all washed up. It won't come back." I put my pan of water up. Here it comes back again, just as pretty as it was the first time. Stayed a couple of minutes and then faded away.

I can't explain it. It done scared me. Right there in the hearth, that corner, it does the same thing. It'll stay in that hearth, and when you scrub it, the prints will still be there. Nowhere else in the house, just in that corner. A girlfriend of mine was here, and she was so scared she went back to Cincinnati.

*Interviewer: Why don't you move?*

I can't seem to leave. I find another house, but the notion leaves me, and I don't want to move.

My son lost an eye since we were here, I lost an eye, my mother had a stroke, and my father got hit by a truck and hasn't been right since. I didn't used to be like this. I don't know what the heck is wrong with this place.

*Interviewer: How long had you lived here before things started happening?*

I don't know, just a short time. But I ain't done nothing, and it ain't running me off.

*Interviewer: Does the silver stuff come up when it's hot?*

About a month before Halloween. People's told me it could be mercury.

*Female, approximately 55, Scott County*

*The house in the above story is a historic building in Georgetown,*

*Kentucky, and was formerly a hatmaker's shop. Mercury was used
by hatmakers to soften pelts.*

## Haunted Cemetery

I live at Bridgeport, and there's a cemetery behind my house. It's an old cemetery for Indians and soldiers which dates back from the sixteen, seventeen, and eighteen hundreds. And beyond the hill—there's two hills right behind my house, and you go beyond the hills—there's a big old house. It's almost completely torn down now from vandalism.

When I was about six years old, if you went back to the house anytime, night or day, you could hear screams coming out of it. You could hear cars starting up when there weren't any cars around, and you could hear doors and windows slamming. You could see the doors or windows were closed.

*Female, age 21, Scott County*

## Shooting Reenacted

In the house where I lived as a child—the house has burned since then—a young girl killed herself. She was very young, and the man she was in love with ran off with another woman.

She shot herself with a gun, upstairs in her bedroom. That was the room my oldest sister slept in. Real late at night, especially on Friday and Saturday nights, around three o'clock, there would be a very loud boom like a gunshot. It was so loud it would wake up everybody sleeping upstairs. There was only one shot. Each time there was only one. I mean, it wasn't two or three shots, but just one.

It only happened about every other weekend, and it was always around the same time. Most times if it happened on Friday night, there would be another shot on Saturday night.

*Female, age 65, Woodford County*

## Knock in the Highboy

When I was just a kid, my daddy bought this old highboy from some woman. Her husband had died, and we brought it home, and we put it in a room in a closet. Great big highboy, and it knocked every once in a while, like something hammering it. My daddy would take it and look at it, never could find why. He always said the wood, swelling in the wood, caused it.

He didn't believe in ghosts. He always had an excuse to get by believing in ghosts. We kept it three or four years, and finally we got tired of fooling with it. Didn't like it, got afraid of it, us kids. My daddy took it and sold it to somebody, got shed of it.

*Male, age 70, Scott County*

## Newspapers Disturbed

There were four of us boys. We had a room upstairs, and right outside was a nightstand covered with newspapers. We were all in bed. We heard the door open, and someone or something came in the door. We heard it come up the stairs, but it stopped by our door. We heard the newspapers rustle on the table outside our door, and that was all.

*Interviewer: Was it the wind that blew open the door?*

No, the front door was closed when we got up.

*Male, approximately 65, Scott County*

## Moaning in the Dark

My story is about a girl who lived in Anderson County in the western part, on a farm. So, as the story goes, one day she was walking home, and her cousin picked her up, kidnapped her, and took her to Louisville. Her cousins kept her for three days, and then killed her, and cut her up in small pieces and put her in a burlap sack. They brought her back to this old road close to her home, and dug a shallow grave and just buried her there.

So people were looking for her, and they found her, I guess maybe because of the smell. One way they found her was that the cows were at one far end of the field close to the fence. One of the farmers noticed that and found the burlap, and then they found the shallow grave. So they put up a shrine in her name and buried her right on the same spot where she was found, but they dug the hole deeper and put bricks around in a circle with a metal fence like a shrine. They put a tombstone up for her, giving her name and her birthday. They don't know when she died, but they put "from the third to the fifth." They put a little verse on the tombstone that said, "God beautifully made her and man cruelly destroyed her," and that "she was a pleasure to be with on earth."

And so the people who live there now think the place is haunted, like the forest and the field is not used in that spot anymore. Now a lot of people from my county go there, and they think it is haunted and scary. Some people say that when you pull off, that something automatically turns your lights off. And on rainy, foggy nights, you can hear her moaning and walking through the brush trying to haunt the place. I went there in the daytime, and it was scary.

*Male, age unknown, Anderson County*

## Rattling of Chains

I remember my father telling me about the haunted house in Carroll County at a place called Warsaw. It was actually called "the Haunted House" by the community. It was a beautiful brick house. My father took me driving past it when I was a boy. He told me that it was haunted. I think the house is probably still standing.

He said that one night he went to investigate the house. He took the deputy sheriff and two or three others, you know, to show their colors. It wasn't too cold, but there was no fire or gas heat. While they were at the house, the noises came around 10:00, 11:00, and 12:00. They began to hear noises upstairs, sounded like chains rattling, hitting, and walking. The deputy sheriff said to my father that it would be alright to check upstairs as he had a gun on him, and there was nothing to fear. So they all went upstairs with a light and a gun, and they searched everywhere but found nothing. They all came back down and sat down. As they were waiting, the noise became louder. It sounded like they were trying to chain someone, and the noise became very loud. But they still found nothing.

That's a true story that my father often told me, and, like I say, I believe the house is still standing there in Warsaw. To my knowledge, no one ever moved in or lived in the house once the tale circulated that it was haunted.

*Male, approximately 65, Scott County*

# Lady in the Bedroom

Our house is not very old. It's, like, fourteen years old, something like that. We do have a ghost in our house, because we built our house on the same spot where there was a former house that was burned by the Indians, killing the people in it. The lady that had lived in that house just kind of stays around our house. We used to hear things like doors slamming and floors creaking. Lights would come on, and there wouldn't be anybody there. It's a pretty new house, so things like this shouldn't happen.

We found this graveyard up on the hill behind our house. We figured it must have been the people that lived in the other house that the Indians burned. They either put up the graveyard in memorial to them, or they were really buried there. The lady's name was Lucretia. I think her last name was Adams, but I don't know for sure. There are several other stories, like that the house had been burned by Union soldiers, and about how a flood came and they drowned in it.

My sister used to talk about how she felt something in her room, so one night when she was gone, I decided to sleep in her room. I woke up, and I just felt something. There was this woman in a long grayish-like dress, with long hair hanging down her back, and she was bending over the bed. I broke out in a cold sweat and everything and just lay there.

*Interviewer: You actually saw this?*

Yes, I saw her. Then I thought, "Well, no, this must be a dream or something." So I just lay there, and closed my eyes, and acted like I didn't see anything, and lay very still. And, you know, it didn't want to do anything to me. And so it was a long time, like a couple hours, and I just lay there very tense and finally managed enough courage to open my eyes. By then there wasn't anything there.

When I told my sister about this, she said that the same thing had happened to her a couple of weeks ago. My sister got married and moved away, and we haven't had anything happen since then, so I don't know whether the lady just liked my sister or what. Anyway, that was the ghost at my house.

*Female, age 20, Fayette County*

## Ghost Pianist

Long ago, we used to go out on Halloween to a house at Ironworks and Newtown Pike. We used to go out there and peek in the windows at a great big old piano that was there. The only thing in the room was the piano. (No one had lived in the house for a long time.) The neighbors around there would say that, at certain times, a lady would come down the steps and play on this piano. We used to get quite a charge out of going out there and peeking in the windows.

*Female, age 55, Scott County*

## Red Spot on the Walk

A woman got her head chopped off on the walk in front of a church. And when it rains or snows, there is always a big red spot there where the incident occurred. I don't know why or how it happened, but the red spot shows up, and many people have seen it.

*Male, age unknown, Clark County*

## Blood Stain on the Carpet

At the Gano Avenue parsonage, there is supposed to be a bloodstain on the carpet on the stairs. And there was supposedly somebody that was hung there, at the church parsonage. It was told by a girl whose father was a preacher at the church.

*Female, age 18, Scott County*

## Shadows in the Window

There is this old house in Owen County, Kentucky, that since I've been a little kid I have known to be haunted. Late at night in the moonlight, it seemed like there were shadows in the window. There were a lot of old bullet holes and broken windows in this old building, and it seemed really spooky.

*Male, age 18, Scott County*

## Strange Sounds

One time my cousin and I were talking out in the backyard when suddenly we heard a baby crying. We followed the sound, and, believe it or not, the sound came out of a well in the yard of this old farm home. The sound of crying kept coming to the top of the well, then moved through the yard, and we followed it. It went around the house, and my cousin and I stayed with the sound. It went to the chimney corner and went into the ground. We didn't hear that sound any more.

Another time we were sitting up with my father, who was ill, and I was sitting beside my father's bed when I heard sounds like rats. I looked, and sure enough I saw five rats coming from the dining room. Each had a hold of the others' tail. They went past my father's bed and me, and then straight for the door. They disappeared through it and never made a mark on the door. We looked at one another, and my father said, "That wasn't rats, *was* it?"

I said, "Invisible ones."

Dad thought a minute and said, "Well, remind Sarah to put out rat poison and get rid of those invisible rats."

*Female, age 60, Harrison County*

## Flickering Candle

An old man who lived in a house beside us in Paris died. The house was boarded up after that. On the nights when it would storm, you could see the old man walking through the house with a candle from room to room.

*Female, age 50, Bourbon County*

## Jack-o'-Lanterns

This is a story that was related to me by my mother. It actually happened to her. When she was in her early teens, she was returning home from a party. They would have parties at different people's houses. Like a group of young people from church would gather at these houses to play games and have refreshments and things.

This one night my mother was driving home in a Model A Ford. She parked it in the garage. The garage was quite a distance from the house on a hill. The house was nestled in a valley between the hills.

It was late at night as she left the garage and started walking down the hill toward the house. As she walked, she saw these lights flickering, just flickering about the ground. When she got close to the house, they disappeared.

She figures that they were jack-o'-lanterns. She never figured out anything else. She was around animals enough to know if they were sheep eyes or cattle eyes. To this day, she still believes that they were jack-o'-lanterns.

*Female, age 20, Scott County*

*The jack-o'-lantern is usually associated with carved Halloween decorations. However, in the spirit world, they are known as "will o' the wisps," spirits that delude or mislead an unsuspecting person, luring the person into danger, or even into death.*

## Death Strikes in a Strange Way

Just after the Civil War, in the little town of Hustonville in Lincoln County, plans were under way to construct a new building for the Christian Church. This is an old town, and it is just about two miles from the site of a pioneer fort, Carpenter's Station. A descendant of the family that built the station lived in a house on that original site, about two miles from Hustonville.

When the church was planning the new building, this gentleman gave an additional offering to construct the steeple on the new building, but it had to be high enough that it could be seen from his home at the station. This was done. Years later, on the night the man died, the steeple was struck by lightning!

*Female, age 59, Scott County*

## Mysterious Ball of Fire

In about 1900, my uncle (a brother to my mother) came home one night. It was raining an' all. He came in and unhooked his horse, and as he did, the little dog came from the house and met him. Little dog kept barkin'. He looked back, and there was a ball o' fire. Just looked like fire! So he would stop, the fire would stop. He'd walk back toward it. It would move back. So he got pretty close to the house, and he hollered for my mother and his mother and father. Anyway, he hollered for 'em, and they all came to the door. So he walked on down, and he got close to the yard. Then he'd turn around, and he'd walk back. And they were watchin' him; all of them was watching this ball of fire.

Finally, he sicced the little dog on it. The little dog just bristled up. He kept on after it, and directly he run back and just grabbed into it. It singed all the hair around the little dog's mouth. He just hollered and run back, and just run underneath my uncle's feet. He couldn't get him out from underneath his feet!

The house sets up high and had a rock wall around the lower side of the yard, a level yard. So he goes through the yard gate and pulls it to and walks up on the porch. When he does, all of them is watchin'. This ball of fire come up to the gate and then just rolled off down the hill to the left and went around the corner. They went to see where it went. When they got there, there was no fire or no ball or nothing.

*Male, age 59, Scott County*

## Occurrences in Twin Creek

I'm here to tell a ghost story that is pretty popular back in Owen County. It's concerning this place called Twin Creek. They say that you can go to the cemetery that's at Twin Creek at night about twelve and see a lot of strange things. They also say that down on the creek there is a light that appears mysteriously at night.

*Female, age 18, Owen County*

## Ball of Fire in a Graveyard

Back when I was a little girl, we lived on Turkeyfoot Road across from a little graveyard. This was an old graveyard, and it was on top of a big hill.

We never did figure out why, but every night, about 10:00, a big light, kind of like a ball of fire, would rise up behind the biggest tombstone and move down the hill across the road. Then it would just vanish!

There was no fire or burnt marks, no noises. It just floated up and then came down out of that graveyard, down the hill and across the road. Even though it happened all the time, we never got used to it. It was really strange.

*Female, age 40, Scott County*

## Foxfire or Ghost?

A highway was being built beside a man's home. The road was torn up for at least a year before it was finished. Next to the road being built, there was a pond and a big woods.

This man had gone to a ball game. Since the road was torn up and it was raining, he had to walk. The night was pitch black, and the rain was pouring down as he walked home after the game.

Through the rain, he saw a light by the pond about fifty yards away from him. It looked like a farm lantern. He thought it was coming from the house in back of the pond, but as he kept walking, he could see there were no lights on in the house. The light wasn't very penetrating in the rain, and it never moved. He just walked around the light, keeping his distance.

When he couldn't think of an explanation for it being there, he took off running through a field on the other side of the muddy road. Later, he thought it might have been the glow, from a piece of decaying wood, he called "fox fire."

*Male, age 40, Scott County*

## Light Outruns Pursuers

My father and his brother and this other guy were sitting in the neighbor's yard, and they looked out into a field and saw this light. So they ran out into the field, and they were looking for it, and it was running in front of them. They were running behind it, and they ran and they ran all over the field and everything, and finally the light disappeared.

*Female, age 17, Scott County*

## A Bouncing Light

My sisters used to go out there on the Grays' farm. Old Miss Brooks and them lived in the big house out there on the Grays' farm. A bunch of the younger children would go out there at night. This old barn they had there, it had a loft or an upstairs to it.

They'd go out there and see a light burning downstairs in one of these rooms or stalls. They'd go out there, and some of them would go in to see if they could find out what it was. When they went in, the ones outside would holler and tell them "It's upstairs!" So they'd go upstairs. Well, it would be back downstairs. It would just sit there and bounce in the window, the light would. But they never were able to find out what it was.

*Male, age 59, Scott County*

## A Christmas Visit

My husband and I were sitting on the couch in our living room a few days before Christmas. It was very cozy. There was a fire in the fireplace, and the only light in the room was from the fire and the Christmas tree lights. We started talking about Christmases when we were growing up. I remember the Christmas Santa left me a doll with real hair.

My husband reminisced about his grandfather, whom he called "Pop." He said Pop was very gruff around Christmas time and did not like Christmas. In Pop's childhood, there had been no money for Christmas, and so he regarded it as a waste.

On a holiday visit to his grandparents in their later years, my husband was naturally very surprised at a change in Pop's attitude. While my husband and his grandparents were Christmas shopping, Pop asked, "Why didn't you get me a Christmas present?"

My husband replied, "I thought you didn't like Christmas."

"Well," he grumbled, "I'd like a present. One of those belts would be nice."

My husband bought the belt and fifteen more Christmas presents before his grandfather's death. Pop looked forward to Christmas from that time on.

While we were relaxing in our living room and talking about Christmas, we both began to smell the distinct odor of pipe tobacco, the really sweet aroma of Prince Albert. My husband's grandfather smoked a pipe and always had this aroma about him. There was always a pipe and a big round red can of tobacco under the tree for Pop in his later years.

No one smoked in our house, and there was no incense burning. We both smelled the pipe aroma several times and in different parts of the house that Christmas. We felt very good about it and have hoped it would happen again, but it never has.

My mother has died since that time, and I miss her very much. Mother always wore perfume and smelled so good. I have often wished I would get a whiff of her perfume, and I would know she was visiting me.

*Female, age 59, Scott County*

# Christmas Ghost

We moved to the north Middletown area because my husband and I wanted to raise our family in the country. We found this pretty Cape Cod house that was built in the 1930s. It was not too far for my husband to drive to his job at IBM in Lexington, and I had a teaching position in Bourbon County.

We were pleased with the house. We had lived there about six months, and we were getting ready for our first Christmas there. Dad was out in the barn stripping tobacco, and my three children and I were starting to trim the tree.

There was the usual hubbub with three excited kids. We started putting bright ornaments on, and every once in a while, someone would say, "OOOH!" At first, I thought it was our youngest, but when my oldest said, "Who is making that noise?" I started watching to see which one it was.

We put on a nice ornament and again we heard "OOOH!" But this time we could see each other, and none of us had spoken. So, it was out to the barn and the stripping room to visit Dad. He was not pleased about our "imaginations running away" with us.

The next night we were putting on the lights, and the kids were not so excited as the night before. We got a strand strung and plugged it in. When they came on, we heard "OOOH!" Well, as one, we headed out to the stripping shed. Dad was not happy with us, but we stayed until he came back to the house with us. "There's no such thing as ghosts," he said.

After that, there were a lot of little things—sounds, things moved, like that, nothing really blatant. When school started up again in January, the kids and I were leaving when my husband came back in from his chores. We said our good-byes, and we left. Soon he went upstairs to shave and get ready to go to IBM where he worked.

He was shaving when he heard the back storm door open and then the back door open and close. He grabbed something and went downstairs thinking someone had seen us leave and, thinking the house was empty, had come in. But he said he thought he'd locked that door.

When he reached the door, he found that it was not only locked, but also bolted from the inside! He said that for some reason it just did not feel right, and the hair on his arms and the back of his neck stood on end.

Soon after that we put the house up for sale. One time a couple was looking at it, and my youngest tugged on my skirt and said, "Mamma, are you going to tell them about the ghost?"

It is a nice house, and we didn't have a hard time finding a buyer. That was three years ago. The house has sold two times since then.

*Female, age 30, Bourbon County*

## House Occupied by Uninvited Guests

My mother-in-law, a Christian woman, said she saw a man standing in my window, but the window was too high off the ground for that to have actually happened. My daughter saw a man in the corner by the window, and both my daughter and my mother-in-law became terribly afraid. My mother-in-law went home the next day, saying she would never visit us again as long as we were in that house. She begged me to please move away from there.

There is something very wrong in this house. I would like to know why this is happening. We have heard people talking and making music. I thought it was on the radio or stereo, maybe kids were playing and the sound was echoing down the valley. (The house is in the valley.) I don't want the house torn down. I could go down there to live and feel safe and happy, although I might cry a lot and wonder what would happen to "it" if the house were torn down. I told my husband that I would like "it" to go wherever I live. He said, "Hell, I hope I never hear tell of 'it' again!"

Women saw men, men saw women; some saw, some felt and heard. When I think of it, I still feel sadness, and when I was there by myself, I felt kindness was with me. When I walked through the house or outside, it was with me, whatever "it" was. It was often seen in the back bedroom, which was my room. Everyone who saw it or felt it got scared.

People tell me they find the experience traumatic and terrifying. I wonder why others feel that way but I don't. No one but myself can stay in the back bedroom, my room. Is "it" my guardian angel? That couldn't be, because other people have experienced these things. (Before we bought the house, another lady started to buy it but changed her mind, although I don't know why she did.)

Upstairs there was a vent, and sounds of footsteps through the house could be heard through it. Several people reported hearing them. When I heard it, I thought it was mice or noises from the wind going through the heaters. This was heard at night when the house was still.

One day I asked my granddaughter if she ever saw or heard anything that upset her when she was in the house. She said, "Gosh yes, Granny! Can't you remember I couldn't sleep upstairs for something walking?"

My grandson told me he saw a woman standing in the corner of my bedroom. She was holding her arms out with the palms down, long fingernails, pale complexion, and long dark hair. I told him he might have seen my mannequin. He said, "No, Granny. You didn't have the mannequin then, and besides, mannequins don't talk. This thing said, 'Get out of here. This is my room. Get out of my room.'" He would not go back in again unless someone was with him. He was only a child at the time, maybe six or seven.

No one but my family has recently lived in the house. It is between seventy and one hundred years old. We have lived there for ten years. I am not a religious fanatic. I just know there is a supreme being, a kind protector who has listened and helped me in my tribulations through my life. I think everything comes from Him, and it is not evil. I try to have a reason for everything, but I can't explain this.

I'll try to explain the best I can what was first told about the house. A neighbor, living approximately three miles below us, would walk to his mother-in-law's house, which was approximately one-fourth mile above us. You couldn't travel the road by vehicle on account of the strip mining that had been done in that district.

This neighbor told my husband he was walking one day and saw a woman turn off the road and walk down the path to our house. She looked up, and when she saw him, she started running. There was a large tree blocking his view for a few seconds, and then she seemed to disappear. There was not enough time for her to get in or around the house. My husband asked him if he looked for her, and he said, "No, but she looked like she was scared." We don't know if he ever saw her again.

My second cousin was at the house after we bought it but before we moved in. He said he didn't see the woman but heard her "holler." He looked around thinking it might be one of us but never saw anything. He said she sounded like someone in distress. Several people said they heard a woman holler down there but never saw her. Some thought it could have been an animal of some sort. There are heavy woods all around there.

I never did hear it. I heard my daughter call "Mom!" once as I was walking toward the house, but my daughter wasn't there. Also, my sister called my name, "Ruth!" in the same tone of voice, at the same spot, when I was leaving the house once. She lived in the state of Oregon at the time. I didn't pay any attention because I know people will hear their names called. I have had that happen lots of times. About two weeks ago, I heard my grandson call, "Granny," and he was in Richmond. Also I heard my son, and he lives in Lexington. I thought they had come to visit me.

My son lived upstairs for a couple of months and said he had a hard time sleeping because someone was walking around all the time. Also one of my granddaughters had the same problem. The sound was coming through the vent above my sleeping room, which was where things were seen. I am not afraid, but I'm getting very curious and will be cautious until I find out something definite myself. I have thought about having someone "bless" the house. Do you think I am weird?

*Female, age unknown, Fayette County*

*The above is a letter from a lady who is genuinely concerned about the manifestations she experienced in her house. She lives in Central Kentucky, but the house in the story, which she still owns, is located in the southeastern part of the state, near London.*

## Woman Senses Presence

After your father died, there were times when I'd, uh, sense him, feel something, you know! This one time, though, we had been sick. I got real sick with the Hong Kong flu. I was just layin' there on the couch. Y'all had gone to school. I was just layin' on the couch.

Then I would feel somethin', like, I could just feel him, my husband, hangin' around. I just knew it, you see. When I'd think about him, I'd see him. Like this one time, I dreamed about him when I was on the couch, and he came. He took my hand, and I would feel the pressure on my hand.

I knew it was him, I saw him in my dream, and then I felt the pressure of him just grippin' my hand—just grippin' my hand, just that tight. I dream about him, and sometimes we'll be talkin'!

I saw him, when I waked, just there! [Informant gestures.] And I felt the pressure just grippin' my hand!

*Female, age 50, Carroll County*

## Ghost Be Gone

They say my house is haunted, but when I hear something, I look over my right shoulder. If you look over your right shoulder, you won't be able to see them; the ghosts will disappear.

*Male, age 81, Jessamine County*

## Animal Revenant

My grandmother could always see things. She'd see things no one else could see. Lots of times she'd see 'em in the shadows around old buildings and cemeteries. This story shows that Granddad saw things too.

One night, she and Granddad were going down the road over in Owen County. Grandma and Granddad were walking, going to Shiloh. She said she could see this thing was in the middle of the road. It was just about the size of a bear but didn't have no head on it.

Well, they had to go on, but it was standing in the road. They was scared, but Grandpa got up close to it. She said Grandpa stopped and took off his coat, and said, "Scat, you scoundrel!" and he kept swingin' his coat at it. Said it never would run. He'd swing at it, and it'd just move aside. He'd stand there and hit at it, and it would just move from side to side. She said finally Grandpa walked on and left it an' they were able to get on home.

*Female, age unknown, Owen County*

## The Ghostly White Dog

I never did see any ghost at all, but one night shortly after dark, Daddy Ben went out. Dad always would go outdoors at night before he went to bed. I was scared by myself after dark in them days, so I wasn't going out because we didn't have no lights at that time down under the hill.

Now it was like being out in the country after you cross the highway and get next to the river, even though it was really in town. Dad went out, and he said he saw a big white dog, uh, about that tall [informant indicates height] an' said it had a big, long bushy tail, and red, fiery eyes. And Dad, he never was a-scared, 'cause he's the type of person that always would see things anyway. I don't know how he is now that he's got one eye bad, but he could always see *things*. He said this big white dog was standing there under that ole cherry tree right at the corner of the house, where Dad had that old Ford parked. That old dog was standing there under the old cherry tree, and dar he was!

He said he could feel the hot air! Said that it was a ghost, a spirit, like 'at. Why, maybe you'd look up and it'd be there, and in the blink of your eye, it'd be gone, and that's what a ghost and a spirit is.

So he said that he saw it standing 'ere and said the hot air hit him in the face. Said the hot air will hit you in the face from this thing. And Daddy Ben said he just kinda hit his hands together, like 'at, and it was gone. Just like nothin', disappeared like nothin'.

*Female, age 50, Carroll County*

## A Terrifying Experience

You know, I have been a Christian all my life, and I don't have a lot of store in a lot of things people claim. But I had an experience once that I don't know how to figure. I wasn't much of a Christian then, but this started my thinking.

I grew up in West Virginia. When I was a young man, I was courting, and I would sometimes walk about three miles to see this girl. One afternoon in summer after dinner, I got cleaned up and started off to see her.

I had walked for a while—the roads were dirt and gravel—watching my feet puff up dust. It was a little later than I usually started, but not too late. I turned off our road onto the dirt road that went to my girlfriend's house. I had a little over a mile to go to her house when I got this feeling to look back for some reason.

So I looked, and several hundred feet back, I saw a shape, a light shape in the road behind me. I figured it was a dog and kept on going.

After a while I looked back, and it was still there, only a little closer. It looked about the size of a pig, and I figured that's what it was. Somebody's old hog got loose on the road. I hollered at it, but it didn't move. It had stopped when I had. I didn't think it was right, but I started off again.

This time I kept lookin' over my shoulder every once in a while. It was still behind me, but it was getting a little closer. I threw a rock at it, but it kept comin'. You know, I couldn't see any feet or legs! I was getting uneasy.

So I started to walk faster, and it'd go faster. The faster I walked, the faster it went. I was not but two hundred yards from my girl's gate, so I ran! And I could run in those days. I was fast. But it kept pace and was gaining again.

I reached the gate at full stride, and I yelled at her Pap. You see, their house set back from the road at the end of a lane. It set on a little rise, and my girl's Pap would always go sit on the porch and watch the road and wave to folks he knew. I also knew he kept a loaded gun just inside the front door.

Well, I commenced to yell, "Pap, get yer gun, get yer gun!" I could see that thing gaining on me. It felt terrible; it made me feel terror. It never made a sound; I never heard a footstep. I could see it just floating on over the ground.

Pap started shooting, and I kept running on up onto the porch. Pap threw another clip in his 22 rifle and fired off a couple more. "Lord," he says, "Jesus Christ, what was that? I seen it chasing you, and I had already got my gun when you commenced to hollerin'."

"I don't know," I said, "but it scared the tar outta me!" We just stood there looking back down the lane. Pap said that the bullets went on through it, but halfway up the lane it just disappeared.

Normally, I'd stay till close to dark and trot off home. Not this time: I stayed over. Pap said it must have been of the devil. I just knew I didn't want to be on the road out there in the dusk! It was some time before I'd walk those roads again, and I'd leave myself lots of daylight. I have puzzled over this experience. I don't talk about it. People might think me "off" a little. But it happened, and I still get chills thinking about it. It made me think more about what the Bible says about demons and devils.

Pap is dead now, but his daughter can verify my story. She's my wife now.

*Male, age 40, Scott County*

## Ghostly Presence Felt

About 1800, three brothers arrived from Ireland. One of them was my great-great-grandfather, Oliver, and he built this place in Frankfort, and the other two, William and George, went to Georgetown and were hatters there.

Then Oliver got the job to design the first statehouse, and for that he was given this land, 485 acres. Oliver and Nancy, his wife, built this house in about 1810 or 1812.

So I went down to Liberty Hall, and I just felt eerie the whole time I was there. I had this feeling somebody was there. I just felt it. I felt very much at home, and I felt as though I had been there before, almost like you'd walked back into another world. I really, really recognized the place. Part of that may have been the era, and our houses being somewhat akin, being built around the same time. Their house was a little earlier, I'm sure. I didn't see anything while I was there, but I certainly did feel it. It's hard to explain what it's like unless you experience it.

*Female, age 50, Franklin County*

*More detailed information about the Liberty Hall ghost will be found in the story "The Gray Lady of Liberty Hall," chapter 10. As for the brothers who went to Georgetown to be hatters: could they be the source of the mercury in "Spirit Comes and Goes," in this chapter?*

# Dark Hollow

In Magoffin County, Kentucky, the road between Salyersville and Paintsville is called the State Road by the local inhabitants. One must leave this road about five miles above Salyersville to begin a long trek to a hidden community of a few houses in a hollow called Pin Oak. From there a road, unused except for wagon and foot, takes you to Burton Fork, which is the left fork of Mash Fork.

Only a few houses existed when my father was born and raised there in 1900. About halfway between Pin Oak and Burton Fork, there is a deep hollow under great timbers. It is always dark there, even in the day. You can imagine what it is like in the night. Three stories stand out in my mind that I heard told, in my childhood, of the "Dark Holler," as it was known.

My grandfather said that one night he was walking alone about 11:00 p.m. Upon approaching the hollow, he heard babies crying. This had often been told to him by others when he was young, but this was his first experience. Many times after that, he heard the same or a similar cry. Others in the community who dared to venture at night also claimed it as a fact. (Often the rubbing of tree limbs will produce this kind of noise when the wind is blowing, but investigation was often made in the daytime to no effect.)

My great-grandfather tells the second story. He too was walking through Dark Holler late at night. The noise of babies crying came to him. As he approached the center of the hollow, a ball of white began to roll down the mountain, across the road, and continued on down 'til out of sight. He said that he took his walking stick, which mountain men often had with them, and poked at the ball as it crossed the road. He told that for a fact all his life.

A third story of Dark Holler was told by my uncle. He said that his daddy and his brother entered the hollow one night. They looked down the mountain into the lagoon, only to see a large figure of light walking to and fro' *over* the lagoon. Was it a gas escaping from the lagoon—sulphur—or perhaps something else? No investigation has ever been satisfactory.

Dark Holler is still there, hardly ever used except perhaps by a hunter or someone surveying the land and the scenery. It is still clouded in mystery; other stories prevail. To my knowledge, no one proceeds to enter it by night.

*Male, age 43, Scott County*

## Restless Residents of Stage Coach Inn

There are several houses within six miles of each other that are over a hundred years old. My aunt happened to live in one of them, the one they now call the "Stage Coach Inn."

Back years ago, in the western expansion days, the stage coach used to stop there. When my aunt lived there, you couldn't sleep upstairs in that house for chains rattling, and steps a-walking up and down the stairs. Doors would slam late at night, or a fire would come up in the stove, maybe a stove door would be left open. . . . It's unbelievable! That's all I can tell you, except it has had many owners.

*Male, age 35, Henry County*

# Ghostly Footsteps

Well, the house we live in now is a two-story house. I've always favored a two-story house. We went through, remodeled, repainted after we was there a couple of weeks. We then started taking the paper off the wall, and just redecorating.

Up to this time, we hadn't heard anything. It was a comfortable house to live in. After we started taking the paper off the walls and redoing it to suit our needs and the way we wanted it, we began to hear noises.

The first time I heard noises, it was like a door rattle. I thought it was my son coming in, because he was out on a date, and he was just coming in. So, I didn't think anything about it, and I went back to sleep. Then my son did come in, and he went upstairs.

So about two o'clock in the morning, I heard someone going up the stairs. I thought it was one of my younger children up, so I got up and went upstairs to look, and everyone was asleep. So I went back down the stairs, and went back to bed, and I heard the walking around upstairs again. So . . . I covered my head up and went on back to sleep.

The next night, I heard the same noise, the same walking up the steps, and I woke my wife up, 'cause I was afraid it was something more than just children. My wife woke up, and she heard the same thing that I did, the door rattling and someone walking up that stairs. There wasn't ever any steps coming back down, and never nothing scary.

So the next morning I told my son about it. Instead of him sleeping up there, he slept downstairs, and we locked the door to his room. That night, my son was sleeping on the couch, and, about two o'clock in the morning, I heard the steps going on up the stairs . . . and the stairs have carpet on them, but it sounded like someone was walking on wooden steps!

I got up to see what was going on. No steps had come down, but the TV came on. We turned the TV off, and, about that time, we heard something in the living room. We went in there, and the ceiling fan was on. I turned it off, and that was pretty much it for that night.

The reason we locked the door was to see why the noises were just going up the stairs and never coming down. So whatever it was was coming to that one room. When we locked the door to that one room, it went through the rest of the house. That's why the TV and the fan were turned on.

Since that time we leave the door unlocked, and the TV and the fan haven't come on. We haven't heard the noise on the stairs, and our son sleeps downstairs.

The house we're talking about has belonged to one family. It's been in the family about 120 years, and no one had lived in it before except that one family. There have been several people die in the house, like Chester . . . and the ceiling fan was put in there for Chester.

*Male, age mid-30s, Henry County*

## A Persistent Ghost

Every night the window would open and close. We would hear somebody come in. Sometimes it would come right into our room where we would be sleeping. One day as we sat in the living room, we heard the footsteps coming. It came into the room, sat down in the rocker, and started rocking.

Another night, as I went to light the furnace, I heard what sounded like someone sawing up through the basement ceiling. Many times we heard noises like this. I finally got enough nerve to go on down to start the fire. When I got downstairs, I saw the saw, but no one was there. I looked up and there was saw marks in the ceiling.

We moved in this house in November. We would have moved out sooner than we did if we'd had the money, and if it was summer outside so we could have been tenant farmers.

*Male, age 35, Franklin County*

## Climbing Footsteps

I lived in this house with my family. Each person in the house had heard what sounded like someone walking up the stairs. When we would look, the footsteps would keep climbing, but there would be no one on the steps. My room was at the top of the stairs. A lot of nights, I would hear the footsteps coming up the stairs and would look out my door to see who was coming. Many times there would be no one unless it was a member of my family coming to bed.

One day my mother was in the upstairs hall ironing when the footsteps started coming up the stairs. When they reached the top, they started coming toward her, but they faded away as they got nearer.

My brother and sister slept in rooms right across from each other. They both had their own cat that slept in their room with them. One night the footsteps were coming up the steps but didn't fade away as fast as they usually did. When they reached the top of the stairs, they started down the hall. Each cat ran to its door, and, as the footsteps passed, the cats hunched up and hissed.

We found out after living there for a while that a young man had lived in the house who was tragically killed in an automobile wreck. He had been decapitated.

*Female, age 25, Harrison County*

## Death Comes for Uncle Natie

I can take you to Oakshire, Kentucky. Nathaniel had certain morals that didn't go with the city. He was very prosperous. The time came, of course, for him to pass, and he became very ill. He was in the bed, and neighbors came to sit with him, a very interesting practice.

The women nursed him and took care of him, but a very strange thing happened at the house. It was an eighteenth-century house, huge, with stairs and closed staircases, and one especially coming down to his bedroom with a door closing the staircase.

The ladies would hear voices coming down the stairs, step by step. Uncle Natie was near death as they heard the noises coming down, but the door wouldn't open. At the last step there was a silence. Uncle Natie would turn in the bed, and the steps went back up the stairs. This happened a number of times before Uncle Natie expired.

The neighbors saw lights flashing on and off before his death. Infidel that he was, non-Christian that he was, the devil was coming to get him.

*Male, age 60, Franklin County*

## Ghostly Noises

A man had been convicted of murder and other crimes in our part of the county. They tried him and took him to Turkey Foot. There, in front of Turkey Foot Church, they hung him with a chain, you know. But his spirit is restless. Many residents of the area, and travelers, have reported strange goings-on at Turkey Foot Church. You could go past there a certain time of night and this chain would rattle, and you can hear footsteps!

*Female, age 78, Scott County*

## Notes

1. J. Allan Danelek, *The Case for Ghosts* (Woodbury, Minn.: Llewellyn, 2006), 109–22.

*Chapter 5*

# Poltergeists

Acategory of ghosts not yet fully discussed is the poltergeist—
mischievous and sometimes malicious ghosts who throw things,
move objects around, and generally create havoc. They are the most
perplexing and violent of ghosts.

The word *poltergeist* comes from the German words "polten"
(to knock) and "geist" (spirit). However, the presence of poltergeists
in the Western world has been noted from Roman times.

One of the most famous poltergeists is the one that came to two
teenage girls, the Fox sisters, who lived near Rochester, New York,
in 1847. The family heard knocking sounds, and one daughter decided to respond with snapping her fingers. The poltergeist answered
back, and the girls and their mother created a code of one knock for
"no" and two for "yes." They asked questions that the poltergeist
answered using this code. When the girls went to live with relatives
in Rochester, the poltergeist reportedly followed. These events were
widely published in the press of the day.[1]

Why a poltergeist haunts a place or a person has not been determined, although the cause for these manifestations has been sought
through the years. Explanations range from the presence of the devil
and demonic infestation to preadolescent emotional conflict, the
sin of a family member, or the activities of a previous owner of the
house. Even so, how a subject would attract the poltergeist is a mystery, because not all similarly distressed people attract a poltergeist.

Another theory is that poltergeists are caused by the repressed emotions of stress or anger in the victim, resulting in psychokinesis (objects being moved without touch). This theory, however, does not explain why a poltergeist will pull the covers off of a sleeping child or beset the new owners of a house. (Another possible explanation is that the distressed person himself is causing the poltergeist-like happenings through psychokinesis that he controls consciously or unconsciously, and this parapsychological theory could explain the pulling off of covers and the "haunting" of the house's new owners.)

Regardless of the cause, to come into your house and find your furniture rearranged, or worse, would certainly make you consider the possibility of moving to another house. To have objects move in your house while you are present most likely would increase your certainty that selling the house would be your only option.

The following stories deal with poltergeists. The reader will recall other stories in this anthology about ghosts who could have been classified as poltergeists, such as those who turned on lights in the house or who yanked the bed covers off. For a much darker and more frightening account of poltergeists, see Chapter 11, "A Ghost Story from the Nineteenth Century."

## Sleeper Disturbed

My mother lived in an old farmhouse that was three stories high. Ever since they bought the house and moved in, there have been stories of numerous ghosts in the house. The most famous story is about one room in the house that you couldn't sleep in because something would pull the covers off the bed. There were seven boys and two girls in that family. None of the seven boys would dare sleep in that room. My mother and my aunt, the two girls, decided they would show the boys up and sleep in the room. It was a downstairs bedroom to the right of the stairway.

They went to bed and to sleep. They were thinking about how they were going to put one over on their brothers. My mother had been asleep for several hours when something woke her up. She realized it was a noise from upstairs. Then she heard what sounded like a ball, bouncing down the steps, that would roll on one step and stop. She lay there and listened to what was going on for several seconds. All the time she was thinking it was the boys. And then she said when it got to the bottom of the stairs, it sounded like it rolled right into her room. Then suddenly she became aware of a form standing at the end of the bed. She still thought that it was the boys so she wasn't afraid. Then she realized that the covers were sliding off her body. She still thought that it was the boys and wasn't afraid. The cover slid off of her again. She started to wake my aunt.

This happened several times, and my mother still didn't realize that it wasn't her brothers that were doing it. The next morning they got up. She started teasing them about trying to scare her, until suddenly she realized that it hadn't been them trying to scare her!

Several years later, when I was in high school, I was lucky enough to know the girl who then lived in that house. She said that even now nobody could sleep in that room, because every time they did, they complained about something pulling the covers off of them.

*Female, age 30, Woodford County*

## Singing Poltergeist

She lives in a house on Delaplain Road. She often hears something moving around upstairs. Many times she has rearranged furniture in the upstairs rooms and come back later to find it moved back. Sometimes at night, she hears someone singing.

*Female, age unknown, Bourbon County*

## Moving Beds

This is about a house my grandparents lived in. They were renting this house, and it seemed to be a good house. However, strange things began to happen once they had settled in. Sometimes one or the other would hear a strange sound, but they didn't pay too much attention to it.

They would hear a door shut, or doors would open and shut

by themselves, right in front of them! Then the strangest thing happened: when they woke up one morning their bed was on the opposite side of the room of where it always sat. This caused them great consternation. And . . . it did not stop. Several times a week, no matter which side of the room the bed was on when they went to bed, they would find themselves on the opposite side of the room when they awoke. The strangest thing is that they were never aware of being moved!

Well, no matter how nice or how reasonable the rent, they were not going to stay there to see what was going to happen next, and moved out after living there for only three weeks.

*Female, age 30, Scott County*

## Blanche Eats the Ham

My poltergeist's name is Blanche, but I haven't seen her in a while. I think she decided to stay with a couple of friends of mine in Louisville who don't have a ghost. She used to do little things. Like, a lot of the time when I would light up a cigarette and be sitting there smoking it, I would look down and in the ashtray would be a freshly lit cigarette. I would be at a party smoking Virginia Slims, and nobody else was smoking them, and then another Virginia Slim would appear in the ashtray.

One time some friends were playing with a Ouija board, and they didn't know anything about Blanche. So I asked them to ask the Ouija board about Blanche, and the board spelled out "poltergeist."

About the last time I personally saw any of Blanche's maneuvers was after a party at which we'd been talking about her. I think she decided to stay at the apartment of two guys who had the party. They said they had a ham in the refrigerator wrapped up in foil, and the next day the foil was in the form of the ham, but the ham had disappeared! None of us had eaten it. I think the spirit stayed with them, because they still talk about the things she does to them, and she hasn't done anything to me in a long time.

*Female, age 19, Scott County*

## Poltergeist Keeps Family Guessing

I'll tell you one incident. My parents both can verify it. There were three of us kids, and we all shared a room. You know how a fireplace has a mantel over it? They had pictures of us all lined up on it. Mother came in one night. All of the covers had been pulled off of us and folded up and put in a chair, and all of our pictures on the mantel had been turned face down on the floor in front of the fireplace.

*Interviewer: What is your explanation for this—the ghost?*

I don't know. I'm not going to try to give an explanation for it. You could give an explanation for it if the covers had not been folded up or anything. But, who would take all three covers off and lay them in a chair? I know Mother and Dad wouldn't have, and we were the only five living there at the time.

There was another incident. We had locked the door downstairs one time when we had company. We were all running around, and all of a sudden the door swung open. Dad went down because he thought it was just the draft that made it come open. He went down, made sure that it was locked, and came back upstairs. About fifteen minutes later, the door swung open again.

It was locked. So my dad and grandfather went downstairs and went all the way past the door and everything to make sure there was nobody down there. There was nobody down there. They locked the door, came back upstairs, and, in about fifteen minutes, it did it again, and for sure it was not the draft. And the door was locked all three times.

*Female, age 18, Owen County*

## Flying Bed Covers

One time when my sister and I went to the lower room of the house, we fixed our bed to go to sleep. We hadn't hardly gotten in bed till the cover came off us and floated to the other side of the room. Then we was terrified, and suddenly the covers came back over to our bed and covered us up again!

*Female, age 60, Scott County*

# Lady in Gray Likes Her Music

This happened to a young couple who are members of my church. The couple wanted a nicer place to live, and they found a very nice older house out in the country. They came to me with this story, and I have their permission to tell it to you.

After they had lived in the house for a few weeks, they started noticing noises. Since it was just the two of them, there was no one else who could make these noises.

*Interviewer: What kind of noises?*

Well, like things being moved, and footsteps. Then, one evening, the light in their room went out. When they checked the lamp, the switch was turned off. The lights would be found turned on in parts of the house they hadn't been in and so on.

One night one of them—the woman, I think—saw a tall, gray figure of a woman. She told her husband. He said he thought that he'd seen her too, at another time, but had convinced himself that he was imagining things. Then they saw her several more times, a couple of times when they were together.

So they asked their landlord about it, as they weren't too happy about being rented a haunted house. He told them that they were the first people outside of the family to live in the house. The figure that they saw was Aunt ———, and everyone in the family knew about her, so he had never really thought of the house as haunted. After a while the couple got used to her and decided to stay.

Recently I asked them about their situation, and they said that everything was fine except for music. It seems they are country music fans, and recently, when they were listening to some music, the station changed to a classical music station. When they changed back to their country music, in a few minutes the station would change again!

*Interviewer: Sounds like a short in the radio.*

Well, yes, but shorts in every radio in the house? That's some coincidence, wouldn't you say?

*Male, age 35, Henry County*

## Strange Happenings at Sunny Slope

The house is on Aiken Road in Woodford County between Midway and Versailles. Aiken Road connects to both Old Frankfort Pike and the Midway/Versailles Pike. The farm was settled by my forebears, circa 1794. The house sits atop an Indian mound, and, because of that, four acres of the property are listed on the National Register, as are the house and outbuildings as well. The farm at one time was called Lovedale, but has been known as Sunny Slope since the early twentieth century.

My pioneer forebears were Richard J. and Elizabeth Shipp. Their youngest child, John, built the house in 1820. He never married. His brother, Richard, sister-in-law Sarah, and their family resided on the property. Richard, Sarah, and John are buried on the farm.

It was the youngest son of Richard and Sarah who took over the farm. He (Thomas), his bachelor brother Seneca, and their Uncle John were all born on the farm and died there as well. I have counted thirteen people in my family who have died in this house.

I don't know who haunts the house, but the possibilities are many! My grandfather's brother died at fourteen years of age from a mishap with a gun. His death was the most sudden. My great-grandfather's sister collapsed at the dining room table and died from heart failure. She was only twenty-six years old. At the time of her death, she had been making out cards for her upcoming wedding. Her seventeen-year-old brother died ten months later to the day from typhoid fever. Most of the other deaths were age related. However, my great-great-grandparents died in their fifties, and my great-grandfather was a robust sixty-two years old when he died from a stroke. His remaining sibling had died at the house at the age of thirty-eight.

Now I have written a slight bit about the people who have passed away in the house, I will tell about a few of the incidents that occurred during my four years of residence. The first day of my arrival, I watched in awe as a wicker rocker on the front porch rocked on its own. I moved to the house in 1983, after my grandma had died.

Prior to her death, a woman named Myrtle lived there to take care of my grandma. Myrtle believed in ghosts. We once saw a latched kitchen locker open, and as we watched, she gave me a knowing smile. The bedroom Myrtle stayed in was across from a room that seemed eerie. Myrtle always kept the door to that room closed because of the spooky feelings that it emitted. I had tried to sleep in that room one night but had to leave because of noises in the wall and an unexplained coldness. My mother slept in there once, and the bed fell! During a Halloween party that I had, my guests roamed the house and were spooked in that room by a feeling of a presence and by the fact that the wardrobe door opened. A psychic that came to the house told me that there had been a murder in that room. I have no way of verifying that, but he was so on the mark with so much of what he felt, that there might be truth to that.

There were humorous incidents during my time there, such as a flip-top garbage can flipping on its own, or a kernel of Kibbles 'n' Bits dog food being flicked across a room. There was the time that I returned from a walk, and I heard a woman in conversation. My mother and I heard a man clearing his throat.

I once heard a knock on the front door. When I opened it, no one was there. There was snow at the door that day, and there were no tracks. I once had a whisk disappear from me while I was using it. I later found it in the kitchen closet.

I will close by telling of a time when a "haunting" was a helpful one. I had once swept the front steps from top to bottom so that the dirt and dog hair were all on the floor beneath the bottom step. When I returned with my dust pan, which I had left the hall to get, all of the dirt—every speck—had disappeared.

*Female, approximately 35, Fayette County*

*After a presentation on ghost stories, the authors received the preceding story, and it is presented here in its entirety in the words of the storyteller.*

## Centre College Poltergeist

Breckinridge Hall at Centre College has a haunted room. It is said that long ago, a young woman committed suicide there. Girls who have lived in this room say that strange things happen there. When they leave the room, upon their return, things have been moved. The chair at the desk has been pulled out into the room or articles of clothing are found on the floor; the closet door is open, and the beds are messed up.

Often when one or both of the girls are in the room, the temperature drops, and it gets very cold. This happens in both summer and winter.

*Male, age 21, Fayette County*

## Ghost Moves Lamp

I had a cousin here at the corner of Oxford and Paris Pike. He used to be what they called a toll-gate man. In fact, when I was about a year old, we lived right across the road. We bought that farm out there. This old toll-gate house, my uncle and them lived there. My cousin lived upstairs.

Years ago, you know, it used to be that you stopped at toll-gate houses and stayed all night. Back in them times, if anybody had money, if they didn't watch, somebody would murder them or something, you see? Anyway, upstairs where my cousin slept, the floor had a big spot of blood on it. Of course you can't get it out of the wood. It stays there. He had one of these little dressing tables sitting there where he kept a lamp. He wouldn't sleep up there without a lamp. Until he died, he swore that something would pick that lamp up and walk around his bed, then set the lamp down at nights. He finally got to where he would not sleep in that room.

It was known, and a lot of people said it was because someone had been killed there. They said if anything like that happens, if you just say, "What in the name of the Lord do you want?" that you'll be answered, and it will quit.

*Male, age 59, Scott County*

## The Bell Witch Haunts a Town

It's an old ghost story. In fact, there is a town named after this ghost—Bell Witch. The story has it that a witch lived in this area, and she died at the ringing of a bell. Somehow, she told the party that rang the bell not to ring it thirteen times. But to spite her, they did, and she died. Then every anniversary of the day she died, that bell rings thirteen times, and she comes back to haunt the people of Bell Witch. She is buried on the farm where she died, and there is a monument and graveyard as well as the small town named after her.

*Male, age 22, Scott County*

*The famous Bell Witch ghost story seems to have originated in the town of Adams, Tennessee, in the early 1800s. A prosperous farmer, John Bell, and his family came under the attack of a poltergeist known as the Bell Witch. The cruel things the family experienced were known far and wide, and were even said to have been investigated by Andrew Jackson, who lived nearby. The story has been retold in the book* The Bell Witch—An American Haunting *by Brent Monahan, and a Hollywood version was presented in the 2006 horror movie titled* An American Haunting.[2]

## Calling up the Bell Witch

Legend has it, if you live in or around Bell Witch, you must stand in front of a mirror, holding a Bible in your right hand and a lighted candle in your left hand, and you must wear a cross. Turn off all the lights and look at your reflection in the mirror, and say, "I hate you, Bell Witch," three times. You will see her reflection in the mirror, then it will fade away as she screams in a muffled tone.

*Female, age 20, Fayette County*

## Rude Awakening

My wife and I were visiting a friend who lived north of the town of Adams, Tennessee. Our hostess gave us her bedroom and went to sleep in another part of the house. During the night, I was awakened by a hard pinch on the shoulder close to my neck. I sat up in bed, immediately awake. Rubbing my shoulder, I wondered why my wife had pinched me. Then I looked over and saw that she was sound asleep.

The next morning, I asked her if she had pinched me during the night, and she was puzzled by my question. I told her what had happened. Our hostess overheard our conversation and she said it must have been the Bell Witch. I responded by pointing out that we were in Kentucky, not Tennessee, where the Bell Witch was thought to be. Our friend replied that the answer was easy. The Bell Witch did not like stories and books written about her and there was just such a book in the bedroom. We all went up to the bedroom to look for the book, but after much searching there and throughout the house, we determined that the witch must have taken it, because the book was gone!

*Male, Age 55, Fayette County*

## The Mysterious Organist and Other Strange Phenomena

A number of years ago, and I don't know exactly what year, I'd say about twenty years ago, we began to hear an organ playing, but we don't have an organ! We just kept hearing these things, just sounded like chords, and it could be any time of the day or night.

No one has lived in this house except my family. The house was built in about 1810. I teased my husband and said it was my Aunt Aggie because I have Aunt Aggie's music books up here. He used to laugh, and the maid would say, "I wish Aunt Aggie would dust all the books in the library, because if she's gonna play, she could at least dust the books she was going to use."

Once, a number of years later, a medium came to the house, and she said she heard music. Of course we couldn't hear the music at the time, and she had absolutely not been told anything about us or our house! Didn't know me at all, or my family. She came up with the initial M, and she sat there and thought and thought. She said, "I believe it's somebody named Molly."

My mother was upstairs in bed, and my husband was going up there to ask her about Cousin Molly. I knew nothing about her, but she's the only Molly I even know. So my husband went upstairs and asked my mother if she had ever heard of a woman named Molly ——, and she said, "Of course. We all called her Cousin Molly." My husband said, "Well, what did she do?" In my mother's generation the ladies didn't do any job, but it turns out Cousin Molly did play the organ for years at the Versailles Presbyterian Church!

I had never heard of that. In fact, I didn't know anything about her. I just knew the name, Cousin Molly ——. So that's all I know about that, but I did ask Mr. H. He said, "Yes, I knew Molly well, and she had played the organ at the Versailles Presbyterian Church, but she didn't play very well." I said, "Neither did the organist who played for me!"

*Interviewer: Do you still hear the organ now?*

No, we haven't heard it but about three or four times since our son Jody died in 1969, and that's when everything started happening. We got to having lots of bumps and things like whistling. Jody used to be a great whistler, and we used to hear whistling around here for, oh, I couldn't tell you, for the longest time.

We used to hear a car drive up on the gravel, and mind you, we have blacktop! But we would hear the car drive up on gravel! (We ascertained that it wasn't next door. We knew that they had a driveway that might have loose gravel, but there wasn't anybody living there that even had a car at that time.) Then we'd hear a knock on the front door. It was so loud one time, my husband, who is a lawyer and pretty much has his feet on the ground, got up and answered the door. It was about three o'clock in the morning.

Estel, my maid, who's been here for years and years, swears things brush by her, and she feels rushes of air like Jody's playing tricks on her. He was that type. He might be whistling and acting like he's in one room while he's really in another.

We heard Jody had been seen walking up and down a Lexington street after he died. All my boys look so much alike, and so many of the kids who knew Jody stayed with us after he died. They would put on his pea jacket and go out walking late. So much folklore has grown up around it, I guess.

Another thing happened right after my son died. I have a sitting room right off my bedroom. Jody was a writer, and he wrote me a lot of letters. I was going through these as I couldn't sleep one night. I was just looking through them, when all of a sudden this cold breeze ran through, and I heard this thump! And at the same time the light kind of flickered, and, man, I put those things down and took off!

The only other major ghosts we've heard are when I've walked into the front door and heard laughter and talking like I'd walked into a party, when I was the only one here.

*Interviewer: How loud is this?*

You know how you might walk into a student union building and you just hear muffled sounds, but not actual words. Then it's just as if the door slammed, and it was no more. I know one Thursday—I don't have any help on Thursdays, no one was here—it was so obvious that I just stood in the front doorway and stood real still and thought maybe I could still hear it, but I didn't. It's as if you tap into waves above your head or above your consciousness.

Then E., who is my third child, when he was about twelve, kept hearing all these women's voices. He sleeps in an old room in the back until he returns to school. It sounded like they were having a party or a meeting, but nothing was there when he looked. Over the years, he got used to them.

In Jody's room, I kept his brush and comb set on the dresser where he left them. One day, and this has happened again, they were moved around. I straightened them out. Later I looked in and they'd been moved again. So I asked if anyone had looked in and had maybe moved things on his dresser. I asked Estel, the maid, and she said no, she hadn't touched them.

Nobody else knew anything about this, and nobody else was home at the time. But it would be like Jody; he liked to tease.

*Female, age 53, Woodford County*

## Slamming Doors and Flapping Wallpaper

My daddy tells us about a house he lived in. They'd hear doors slam. They'd get up and go look, and nothin' would be there. I've heard him say, too, the door would open, and they'd get up and go shut the door. They'd no more than sit down, and it would open again. They moved out of that house because they couldn't keep the doors shut. He said the paper would even come loose from the wall and flap backwards and forwards.

*Female, age mid-30s, Scott County*

## Ghostly Pranks and Music

There was this large house, kind of secluded from other houses, that we had rented. We moved in, and on the first night we went to bed, my wife kept saying, "Quit!" and I said, "Quit what?" She said, "Quit hittin' my butt!" I said, "I wasn't hittin' you on the butt." We turned over, and I felt something run its hand down my face. So we jumped up out of bed and left the house.

We went over to my father's and got my nieces and two sisters to go back to the house. It was rainy, and a scary-like night out when we went back to the house. So we went in and went back to bed. There was a piano in the other room on the right side of the house, and it started playin'. There was nobody in there to make it play; it just started playin'! So we got scared and left the house again.

When we got back to my father's house, he assured us that there was no ghost, and the house wasn't haunted. So we went back in the house, and it was just like this icy feeling, and you'd get goose bumps all over you. We all slept in one room, together, or tried to. The music started to play again. We left the house again and never went back.

I guess a couple of years later, another couple moved in the house, and we discussed what had happened there. They said that they themselves had run into this ghost, and that the piano started playing, so they took an axe and chopped up the piano. That night that they had chopped the piano up, one of the boys looked toward the bedroom where the piano had been. They saw some smoke go through the keyhole! They moved out of the house.

The house is at Campellsburg. No one has lived in there since. You'll *try* to stay overnight in that house, but you will *not* spend the night!

*Male, age mid-30s, Henry County*

# Notes

1. Felicitas Goodman, *How About Demons?* (Bloomington: Indiana University Press, 1988), 33–34.

2. Rosemary Ellen Guiley, *The Encyclopedia of Ghosts and Spirits* (New York: Facts on File, 1992), 35–38.

*Chapter 6*

# Communication with the Dead

Meetings for the purpose of bringing a paranormal communication to a group or to an individual, usually through a medium
of some sort, have been recorded since as early as the third century
B.C. by Porphery. Séances became very popular in the mid-1800s.
Two or more persons (but usually less than eight) would gather
around a table and try to make contact with a deceased loved one
through the medium. The participants were to sit in a circle with
their hands placed flat on the table. Strangers were looked on with
suspicion; their disbelief, it was feared, would hinder the success of
the séance. Music would often be played, and lighting was usually
dim. Skeptics would say the music and dim light could be used to
hide a fraud.

The séance became very acceptable in the Victorian age and on
into the early twentieth century. Henry Houdini was involved in the
spiritualist movement of his period. He was obsessed with a need
to speak to his dead mother and attended many séances. Being an
escape artist, he knew the tricks of hidden lights and mirrors, and
knew many ways of creating manifestations of a "spirit." He dis-
credited several popular mediums but had little success in reaching
his mother.[1] The true believer might say his own skepticism caused
this failure.

In the early 1920s and 1930s, the Ouija board became a popular tool for telling the future or communicating with the dead. It
was invented in 1892 by Elija J. Bond and became very popular after

World War I when multitudes of bereaved parents were trying to communicate with their lost sons. It is still being marketed today (now with a glow-in-the-dark game board!) by the Parker Brothers game company, which states that it is for entertainment only.[2] Nevertheless, it is still being used for ghost sleuthing, as in the story "Coed Returns to Transylvania," in chapter 8.

The photos included in this chapter of the group of students at Georgetown College who called themselves the Mystic 13 (circa 1917) show that there was some interest in the occult at that time at the college. The photo showing the thirteen students wrapped in white, all wearing black blindfolds and grouped around a skull and crossbones, would particularly indicate something of the sort.

The stories in this chapter describe communication with the dead. This may be in a séance where the communication is deliberate, but often it is not solicited, surprising and possibly frightening the recipient of the communication. This communication takes different forms, such as being physically touched by what seems to be a ghost or by hearing a knock in response to a question. Some ghost stories presented in other chapters could fit into this category as well.

## Pleading Ghost

After he died, he said, "Don't leave me; please don't leave me."

I was mad at him; he was steppin' out on me, see, and so then I said, "What about her?"

He said, "Oh, there's nothin' to it, but I have no recompense whatsoever, but please don't leave me."

I just got up. I was so insulted. I left him, the ghost and all. He came back to me. They come just like a shadow.

*Female, age 70, Scott County*

## Grandfather Returns

My grandfather died the day I was born. The first thing I can remember that was weird, I was between five and six years old, somewhere around that age, and at night I'd get up and play. My mother would

The Mystic 13, a Georgetown College student group, 1905–1917. (Courtesy of the Development Office, Georgetown College, Georgetown, Kentucky.)

Another view of the Mystic 13 of Georgetown College, 1905–1917. (Courtesy of the Development Office, Georgetown College, Georgetown, Kentucky.)

even leave food out for me because she knew I used to get up in the middle of the night and play. I can remember that I had a playmate. I can't remember exactly how it looked, but it was larger than I was. It never spoke, but we played together until, one night, it got up and stood in the middle of my bed. I guess I was too tired to play. I kicked it, and it still wouldn't leave me alone, so I went to get in the bed with my parents. I went to get in their bed, and it grabbed me by the foot. I was right next to my parents' bed, and I screamed. My father turned the lights on. It was gone, and that was the last time that I ever saw it.

Then when I was about eleven years old, one night I woke up and there was a man standing at the foot of the bed, and he patted my foot. It was a man I'd never seen before, and I just, you know, screamed, and he just dematerialized. That winter my grandmother came to stay with us, and she had a picture of my grandfather, and it looked very much like the man that I saw that night.

Then when I was about sixteen, one night I woke up, and there he was, looked like the same man. He was putting one of my shoes on my right foot, and I screamed again. He more or less just smiled, and, from what I can remember, he floated through the ceiling.

And at night once in a while, during that year and a couple of years after, I could be sleeping and I'd hear steps across the room, someone sitting in a chair with deep breathing. I'd jump up and turn the lights on. There was nobody there. My grandfather died of lung cancer, and during the last months of his life, when he breathed, he breathed very deeply.

*Male, age 20, Fayette County*

## Knocks from the Chest

My father died. My mother gave all my daddy's clothes to my grandmother, because she didn't want them around after my dad passed away. They were sad. My grandmother took them upstairs and put them in a wooden chest. One night she was awakened, right after she put the clothes in the chest, by a real hard knocking. She raised up in the bed, and she looked all around to see what it could be, and she realized it was coming from the chest. She didn't do anything about it that first time.

The next night she went to bed, and, after she was in bed awhile, knocking sounds started in the chest again! It would knock real loud! So my grandmother just raised up, and she knew it was coming from that chest, and she said, "Is that you, John? If it is, knock [so many] times." It did knock just that amount of times. One, two, or three; I don't know which. She said, "What do you want me to do with your clothes? Do you want me to get rid of your clothes? If you do, knock, [so many] times." It did. She gave his clothes away. That chest is still in the house. She never heard another sound.

*Female, age 60, Scott County*

## Family House Still Occupied

(Part 1) I began to work on the house in the spring. I felt a certain kinship for it since it was the home of my ancestors, deceased long before I was born. My great-great-grandfather built the house for his family of nine children. The more I worked on the house, the more I thought about the type of life my ancestors lived in the mid-1800s.

After six months of hard labor the house was finally livable. I even had running water in the house for the first time ever, new wiring in half the structure, and five rooms nearly completed.

The first weekend of May 1981, I decided to move in because my best friend from college was coming to visit. I was really pushing it to move before she arrived, so it turned out to be the first night that I actually spent in the house. I'm glad someone else was in the house with me to witness the happenings of that night.

We stayed up talking until almost one o'clock. My friend had driven almost all day and she was tired, so we decided to turn in for the evening. I turned all the lights out in the house except the nightlight in the bathroom. The house was strangely quiet after the hammering all week and workers going in and out all the time.

Suddenly, a clanging noise broke the silence. Immediately we tried to figure out what the noise could be and where it was coming from in the house. I whispered to my friend that it sounded like a piece of metal banging on the iron post of my bed. Her wide eyes and strange expression answered for her without a word. Then it stopped as suddenly as it had begun. I turned the light on beside the bed. Everything looked normal. We settled back down to try to sleep after exhausting all the possibilities of the strange sound. The night was quiet again.

I lay there for a long time without falling asleep. The silence was interrupted again; this time I thought I heard footsteps going up the stairs. I didn't want to alarm my friend, so I didn't say anything.

"Did you hear that?" she asked.

"I was hoping you didn't," I said. "I guess I should check it out to make sure no one's in the house."

"I'm going with you; I'm not staying here alone."

I grabbed my field hockey stick. It was the only thing that I had in the room that I could use for a weapon.

"I feel better now," said my friend sarcastically. "Don't you have a gun?"

"Are you kidding? I hate guns. Let's go before I lose my nerve!"

I really wasn't that scared at this point. I thought we would walk out, find an explanation to the noises, and go back to sleep. I was more or less having an interesting evening so far. I peeked through the crack in the door out into the hallway. I was surprised and somewhat puzzled to find the light turned on at the top of the steps. I was starting to get concerned that maybe there really was someone in the house. I shut the door and turned back into the bedroom.

"Now that's really strange," I said.

"I've already got a strange feeling," she said. "I'm beginning to think this house is haunted, all jokes aside."

You know how that human factor of curiosity won't let you just shut the door, lock it, and wait until the safety of the morning light appears to investigate? Just like in a cheap movie, I had to find out what was at the bottom of this little mystery. I opened the door for the second time, hockey stick in hand, heading for the light at the top of the stairs.

We stepped quietly up the stairs. I was leading the way, holding my weapon in a ready position above my head. My friend was very close behind me. It felt like she was hanging on the end of my shirt.

"I know I turned that light off before we went to bed," I whispered. "It's the only light in this wing of the house that works at all."

"Maybe it has a short in it."

"I just had an electrician check it over, but I guess they could have missed something," I added, trying to give her explanation the benefit of the doubt.

We reached the light. I turned it off, then on again. There didn't seem to be anything wrong with it, but a short was a possibility, I surmised in my own mind. "I'm going up on the landing to check out the rooms while I'm up here; you can wait here if you like," I whispered, not wanting to be heard by anyone who might be hiding in the upstairs of the house.

"No way. I think we should stay together."

"Good idea," I said quickly, not wanting to go alone.

We walked past the light, up three steps to the second balcony, and opened the first door. I found nothing. Without a word, I walked to the next door. Again I found nothing disturbed. I reached the third door; it was slightly open. I got that sinking feeling in my stomach, the one that runs down to the pit of your belly, then climbs up your neck, and sticks in your throat. I wondered if I really wanted to look into that room. I had to, though. I pushed the door open and shined the light into the room. Nothing had been disturbed, and there was no one in the room. "Now what?" I turned and asked my friend.

"Maybe the house is settling."

"I don't think 150-year-old houses settle; besides," I added, "I've never heard of lights going on and off because a house is settling."

"What do you think it is?"

"I don't know," I answered quickly. I shut the door, and, as I started to leave, the door began to vibrate. I opened it and shut it again; it was still vibrating. "I think that's just the air current. It must be getting windy outside." These old house are built with studs that go from the ground all the way up to the roof. There are no wind blocks between the outside and interior wall and no insulation to stop the air flow. "The draft between the room and the hallway is so strong it must be forcing the door to vibrate like that. I'll jam the door and stop the air current, and maybe we won't hear any more strange noises tonight."

I was proud of my explanation of the vibrating door. I had learned a lot about the construction of the old house in the past six months. It was logical and believable. I busied myself fixing the door. I placed a four-by-six piece of drywall against the door, then stacked several paint cans in front of it. The drywall was heavy, and the paint cans were full. The door had stopped vibrating.

On our way back to the bedroom, both of us double-checked the light to make sure it was off. I turned it on and off again to make sure it was still working properly. We walked in silence the rest of the way down the stairs.

We talked for a while after reaching the safety of the bedroom, trying to make sense of what we had heard and seen. We couldn't come up with any believable explanations for the light, the strange noise, or the footsteps. We finally gave up and went to sleep.

The next morning the sun was shining brightly through the window. I woke up without hearing any noises. I thought maybe I had been dreaming. I got up and went to the bathroom. I glanced up at the hall light to make sure everything was normal. The light was the way I had left it. I came out of the bedroom and met my friend. "Everything looks OK," I said, as I put my shoes on. "I'm going up-stairs to check on things in the daylight."

"Wait a minute, and I'll go with you."

Everything looked normal until we came to that last door. We both looked at each other, just like we had the night before, and didn't say a word. I was registering everything I was seeing in my brain. Finally, I broke the silence.

"I can't think of any logical explanation for this that makes sense, can you?"

She answered by shaking her head and staring at the scene in front of us. The drywall that I had so carefully placed between the paint cans and the vibrating door had been removed. It was sitting against the window on the opposite wall, four feet away from where I had left it. The paint cans hadn't been disturbed. The door was still closed, no longer vibrating.

"I wonder who moved that drywall?" I asked my friend, willing to hear any explanation she had to offer, since I couldn't think of one myself.

"I think you have a ghost," she said, finally.

"A ghost?" I repeated. "Maybe someone came in this morning and moved that drywall to get into the room."

"It's 7:30 in the morning. Who would be up here, and why didn't they move the paint cans? They are a little high to step over. Besides that, what was going on last night with the light, the strange noise, not to mention the footsteps that we both clearly heard? You better face the facts: I think you've got a ghost!"

"I don't know. There is more than likely some logical explanation to all of this. I just can't think of it right now. If it's a ghost, maybe it's my great-great-grandpa wandering around to see who has moved into his house," I said sarcastically. "Interesting concept, but I won't believe it until I see it for myself," I added.

Every time my friend called me from that time on she always asked me if I had heard from great-great-grandpa. She was convinced that there was a ghost in the house. I have to admit that I was pretty uncomfortable for the next couple of months. I would go to my room at night and stay there until morning. Six months passed, and I didn't hear or see anything out of the ordinary. Things usually seem better after the passage of time. I never figured out how that drywall was moved. After a while I put it out of my mind for the most part, but I'll never forget what my friend and I experienced that night. No matter how hard I tried, I couldn't explain it; therefore it was best just not to think about it at all.

(Part 2) I wasn't convinced until two years later that there might be a presence in the house besides myself. It happened on a cold winter night. It was forty below zero with the wind chill factor. I was sleeping on the couch in the den, keeping a fire going in the old fireplace. It was so cold I had let my dog in the house. He was sleeping at the foot of the couch.

The den and kitchen were separated by a half wall and the brick chimney. The other side of the fireplace was left open so you could see all the way into the kitchen. It was a clear night with an almost-full moon. I could see the big kitchen windows from where I lay on the couch. They were bright with light. It was so bright I had a hard time falling asleep.

I must have finally dozed off because I was awakened by what sounded like a pig squealing. I realized it was my dog. I looked up and saw a tall dark figure standing over the couch. My first reaction was that someone had broken into the house and they were standing over me. I tried to move; my body was frozen. I had never felt that kind of fright before. I was literally scared stiff. The dog didn't move either. His behavior was totally out of character, as he usually barked at anything that moved. I called him my "yap yap" dog, but now he was lying very still and disturbingly quiet, a dead weight on my feet.

I lay there, motionless, with my eyes fixed on the tall, dark figure. I could see a person's outline wearing a cloak-type garment that was dark and reached the floor, but I couldn't make out any features in its face.

The figure began to move alongside the couch. It didn't turn and walk like a person, but moved without effort. The figure seemed almost frozen itself, moving away from me without any human mechanics of leg and arm motion. When it reached the foot of the couch, I could see the brightness of the kitchen windows behind it. It appeared to be a shadow, darker than the night. It moved with a slow and easy speed that never changed. It passed by the window, and I couldn't see it anymore. I had the feeling that it had passed through the door at the end of the couch a few feet away from me, but the door never opened or closed. The figure just drifted out.

I felt my heart start beating again. I could feel it thumping in my throat. I lay there for a few more minutes before I tried to get up. The dog still hadn't moved. I couldn't believe what I had just witnessed. This time I had actually seen a presence of some kind that couldn't be explained by human logic, and so had my dog. I finally regained my composure, and sighed with relief when I could once again will my limbs to move.

This visual contact altered my opinion about the other unexplained things that had occurred in the house. I still don't know exactly who or what the presence was standing over me. I have no idea if it was just watching, or trying to communicate, or if I had just caught a glimpse into a different dimension of time (if such a thing exists). I would no longer wonder about the drywall, the footsteps, or the mystery of the hall light. These were trivial compared to the unexplained presence that had visited me in such an unorthodox manner.

To this day, all I know for sure is that both the dog and I saw the presence standing over us. Therefore, whatever it was, the animal world as well as the human world was affected. I have no real knowledge of the true identity of the presence. I don't know what ghosts are, much less supernatural spirits, or whether they are made of fact or fiction. It was an unexplained presence that didn't communicate or make its identity known to me. It has crossed my mind that I was too scared for it to communicate with me. Sensing this, it might have gone on its way. That's what I would like to believe.

I can't erase the dog's squeal from my mind. I don't think humans hear that particular sound in the domesticated dog very often. I never had, and I have had dogs all my life. It was a wild, horrid sound that jolted me out of a peaceful sleep. If I could have forgotten that sound, I probably would have clouded the incident over with philosophical logic in self-defense.

For some reason this incident gave me the feeling that I had been accepted by the presence that seemed to be associated with the old house. I felt more secure after actually sighting it. I tried to think of it in context with my ancestors; maybe it could be great-great-grandpa trying to let me know that he was glad I was there trying to fix his house. That's the way I like to think of the presence. Regardless of what it is, it didn't hurt me.

The presence also managed to open up a Pandora's Box for me on the subject of the existence of supernatural spirits. Today to that puzzling question, "Do ghosts exist?" I would have to answer, "Anything is possible," and then add, "Some of us have to deal with personally catching a glimpse of the supernatural world."

(Part 3) I was married in October of 1988. I moved out of the old house for nearly two years. My husband and I moved back in November 1990, after more renovation and the birth of our first son. I didn't hear or see anything out of the ordinary for almost two weeks.

Then, one evening when we were sitting in the family room watching the evening news, we heard footsteps walk across the floor in the bedroom above us. The footsteps were definitely made by someone wearing hard-soled shoes. We went upstairs to check things out, but we found nothing. There was no one in the house. It troubled my husband more than it bothered me. It was the first time he had heard the "night walker." Maybe the presence was saying, "Welcome home"; at least, that's how I like to think of it.

Since then we have a new cry in the night. My husband tuned in to this unexplainable sound first. He said he heard a newborn baby crying, as clearly and distinctly as if it were in the room with him, but it wasn't one of ours. He would hear it periodically at different times of the evening. I didn't hear it for months. Finally I heard the cry as my two sons slept soundly in the room where we were sitting. I have learned to live with the oddities in this house. A cry in the night: another unexplained sound from the walls of this house that has seen many different generations.

*Female, age 25, Scott County*

*This informant told the authors that many years ago a farmer had committed suicide at the site discussed in the above story, and her grandfather had died of a heart attack in the house. Readers may draw their own conclusions as to whether these deaths have any relevance to the events that later occurred there.*

## Mom and the Haint

My mother lived in this house when she was fifteen. They had rented the land this house was on for three years. They couldn't keep the windows and doors shut. Up in the attic there was this big wardrobe, and it would sound like it fell over, but when they got up there, the wardrobe would still be standing up. The people who had lived in this house before them had two girls who slept up in the attic. These girls said they had seen something fly out of the wardrobe and out the window. It was kind of human looking. It was a transparent mass.

One day my uncle was lying on the sofa with the window open looking out of it. As he looked out the window, this kind of transparent mass, like the girls described it, flew out of the ditch across the road toward him. He felt it was coming after him and was going to hurt him. He started screaming. Everybody in the house rushed in there, and he was hysterical, but they didn't see anything.

One day the girls were coming up the lane to the farm. As they were coming up the lane in view of the house, they saw an old lady going in the front door. They thought it was their grandmother. When they reached the house, they asked where their grandmother was, and their mother said, "She's not here." The girls asked, "Who was it who came in the house?" and she said, "Nobody's been here." So the girls searched the house, and there was no old lady there.

After the first year when they had gotten their crops in, they were planning on moving because of these strange happenings. Their last night in the house, the men had gone in to town and my mother, being the oldest, was in charge of the other kids. They all slept out in the living room. The kids were all excited, making a lot of noise, and wouldn't settle down and get to sleep. My mother told them to settle down many times, and they just kept on. So she told them if they wouldn't be quiet, she was going to call the Haint on them. "Haint" is what they called the thing that haunted the house. The children kept on making noise, so my mom said, "Come on, Mr. Haint," and all of a sudden the door flew open and hit the bottom of

the bed where the children were lying. Then there was dead silence
in the house. Finally my mom got up enough nerve to shut the door.
That was the last experience they had with the haint. They came to
find out that a traveling salesman had been murdered in this house
and they never buried him. They just threw him in the river behind
the house.

My brother, when he was in college, decided to go back to the
old house and look at it. At this time he was running around with a
guy who claimed to be a warlock. He took this guy with him. When
they reached the place where the house was, it had been torn down.
As they stood on the site where the house had been, his friend, who
had never been there, told him exactly the same story of the murder of the traveling salesman and how they had thrown him off in
the river. As far as anyone knows, he had never heard the story before and didn't know the location of the house until they had gotten
there.

*Male, age 43, Shelby County*

## Lights in the Attic

An acquaintance of mine bought a house in Lexington and was en-
joying living there until a neighbor asked what they did up in the
attic every night. My friend told her that they never went up to the
attic at night, but the neighbor insisted that the attic light was coming on late at night and staying on for some time. But the light was
always off by morning. My friend could find no reason for this to
happen. The wiring was not defective, and the light switch was OK
and so forth.

Finally, she and her husband heard of a lady in Lexington who
was supposed to be able to get in touch with the dead, and although
they were skeptical, they made an appointment to see her. To make a
long story short, she told them that the previous owners of the house,
who had died several years ago, were returning to the house to see
if everything was all right. If their visits were disturbing the present

owners, they wouldn't do it anymore. The lights in the attic never came on by themselves again.

*Female, age mid-30s, Fayette County*

# A Shocking Phone Call

My husband and I came to Georgetown one evening to eat at the Golden Corral. While we were eating, I had what we thought was a heart attack.

I was rushed to the Scott County Hospital emergency room. I was there several weeks because they found my heart to be sound, and they were carrying out tests to find my problem. It was touch-and-go for a while, but they finally determined that I had a toxic reaction to caffeine. I was then allowed to go home to Bourbon County to recuperate.

I am the youngest of five sisters, and we have always been close. I was always especially fond of my oldest sister. She had been an art-ist and a writer, first in New York, then in Chicago. No matter where she was, she always thought of me, and I of her.

One nice sunny morning [after the heart episode] I was sitting up in bed reading when the telephone rang. I wasn't allowed out of bed yet, so the phone was at my elbow. When I answered a woman said, "How are you?"

"Better," I said. "Who is this?" But she just went on and on ask-ing me a lot of questions. I asked again, "Who is this?"

"Oh, you know," she said, and then asked me about my sisters. She then asked me about something when I was a little girl. This time I said, "Who *is* this?!?"

She replied, "You know, I'm your sister ——!"

It was just like I'd had an electric shock. It went all through me when I realized it was my favorite sister. I hadn't recognized her voice at first; it had been so long since we'd talked. She had died ten years ago.

*Female, age 40, Bourbon County*

# Dead Supper

A dead supper is a ritual to bring back spirits. Mr. C. said his grandmother brought back her own mother's spirit by performing such a dinner ritual. To accomplish this task, everything in the supper is prepared backward. Then the supper is served backward. Mr. C.'s grandmother's mother appeared at the end of such a supper, and his grandmother fainted.

*Male, age 65, Scott County*

# Notes

1. Rosemary Ellen Guiley, *The Encyclopedia of Ghosts and Spirits* (New York: Facts on File, 1992), 169.
2. Ibid., 239.

# Chapter 7

# Ghosts That Weren't Ghosts

One fact became quite evident to all those who collected stories for this anthology: people like to discuss the subjects of death and ghosts. Telling stories around the campfire (or in similar gatherings) has always been a great pastime, particularly when the atmosphere is just right. Consequently, some stories were collected that did not directly involve ghosts but were related. Some might be considered "scary stories," others are about "sham" ghosts, and some are experiences with death.

The fear of being buried alive is quite common and is the basis for many scary stories, including "Buried Alive?" in this chapter. Before embalming was a common practice in this country, there were reports of "corpses" reviving. This occurred when persons who were thought to be dead—but who were actually in a coma or trance—were laid out and about to be buried. In the worst cases, the burial actually took place before the unfortunate person's awakening. Rarely, these people would be able to break out of their graves; most often they perished in their coffins after a desperate struggle to escape. Of course, people wanted to be sure this did not happen to them! Various devices intended to avoid this fate were marketed, such as a voice tube that extended from the inside of the coffin to the surface of the ground. There was also an apparatus, the Bateson Life Revival Device, that had a cord inside the coffin, attached to the corpse's fingers, that led to a bell above the grave.[1]

Sometimes "ghost" stories turn out to have perfectly logical explanations, as in the "Ghost or No Ghost" and "Ghost with Chains" stories in this chapter. This can be very disappointing to someone who has enjoyed telling the story to friends and family.

Stories with many details that are repeated, such as "Scary Situation" (following), are the kinds of stories that might be told by a father to his family while sitting by a campfire on a warm summer evening and then perhaps repeated by his child at the next sleepover with friends. They aren't usually meant to be believed and often follow the tradition of "Where's My Golden Arm?" and other campfire stories that invariably end with a loud exclamation to startle and scare the listeners. (A storm or heavy rain outside helps to set the scene and increase the effect.)

## Scary Situation

A friend of mine from Lexington was making a trip on a train. As he traveled along, he could not help but notice that the person across the aisle was very nervous and evidently irritable. After observing his neighbor's chain-smoking for quite a period of time, and noticing his shifting about in his seat and his glancing around repeatedly, my friend began to be very concerned. He decided to get a breath of fresh air, and, to get away from the nervous man, my friend went to the back of the train and out onto the observation platform.

As the train clicked along, he realized that the door to the car had opened, and the man across the aisle had come out on the platform too. He began to move back and forth, still in a very high nervous state. Finally, he came to my friend and he said, "I've got something I just have to say. I've got a story that I have to tell you. I need somebody to help me, and I wonder if I can tell you my story and you'll help me." The man told this story:

He said when he was in college, his fraternity prepared to initiate new pledges. He said each year the fraternity tried to find a more severe way, a way that would frighten pledges more than in previous years. He said that in his senior year he was chairman of the committee, and that it was his responsibility to select the most difficult place, the most harrowing experience, and put the pledges through this. So he said, "I sought a place that we might use, and I finally discovered that out in the country was an old, deserted house, supposedly a haunted house. We developed a plan, and we waited for the blackest night to take the pledges to this haunted house and carry out the initiation procedure. On the night when we decided to make the effort, we took all the pledges and our members out to the field near this haunted house, and we went through the procedure we would follow."

Each pledge was to pass through a field of weeds, where the others could hear the crackling and rustling of them breaking the stems, then they were to go to the corner of the house and climb up a gutter pipe, cross the porch roof, come in through an open window, cross an up-stairs room, come down the stairs, knock three times on a door at the foot of the stairs, and then reverse the process and return to the group. "And so," he said, "we sent the first pledge and we could not help but hear the weeds crack, we heard the gutter pipe creak as he climbed up it, and we heard him walk across the porch and into the upstairs window. We heard the boards creak as he went across the floor, and we heard the stairs as he made the descent. When he got about halfway down, we heard a sort of a thud, and no other sound was made.

"Well, we decided to send the second pledge, because evidently the first decided to go along with us and make it worse for the rest of them, and so this tied right in with what we planned. The second person was obviously frightened and nervous, but he started across the weed patch, climbed the gutter pipe, crossed the porch, climbed through the window, crossed the room, and went down the stairs to about the midpoint, and there was a screech, a muffled cry, and no further sound.

"We decided to send the third pledge, thinking the first two had decided to make it rougher on those that followed. He followed the same procedure, and we heard him go up the pipe, across the porch, through the window, across the room, and down the stairs, and there was just a cry, a screech, a thud, and again no more sounds.

"Being chairman of the group, I decided, 'Well, this will never do. They have just ganged up on us, and it's not really going to work; it's backfired.' So we all decided we would go to the haunted house and take out the first three pledges or else they would ruin the initiation for the rest. Just to do as the others did, we too went through the weed patch. We decided to climb the gutter pipe, and I waited, being the first up, till the others got to the top of the porch. Then we all went through the window, across the upstairs room, and, since I was in front, I started down the stairs. Just as I got about midway, my hand was rubbing along the dark wall, and I felt something cold and clammy and round. I could tell in a moment that it was a doorknob. On the stairwell, without my remembering it, was a door. My hand clasped the doorknob, and it turned.

"The door opened, and I looked inside a small room and saw there a table with a lighted candle on it. I saw the outline of the first boy we had sent in, lying on the floor. I saw the second boy we had sent in, who was in a daze, staring, and he seemed to be very rigid." Then he said of the third boy, "I couldn't believe what my eyes told me. The third boy was completely gray; he had hold of the arm of the second boy that we had sent in."

Then the man said to my friend, "You know all of us became very concerned, because every year since then something terrible has happened to one of the members of the committee that was responsible for the initiation of those pledges in that haunted house." Then he said, "You know, this is my year, and I think I'm going. . . . *M A D!*"

*Male, age 47, Scott County*

## Sham Haunting

I know a man whose father's house was supposed to be haunted. They would hear strange sounds at night like a body being dragged, and chains rattling. This went on for some time, and people talked about that house being haunted. Then one night they caught these two boys, dragging chains across the porch floor.

*Female, age unknown, Harrison County*

# Buried Alive?

This young lady died, and they buried her, and she hadn't been dead very long. They wanted to change her burial place. They took her up, to move her to another cemetery, or another burial place. They opened the casket to see for sure that it was her. Said she had both hands clinched in her hair.

*Female, age mid-60s, Scott County*

# Family in the Deep Freeze

Well, this was back in Knott County in the 1930s or '40s. When these here people lived back there, well, the people just bred and bred and bred and bred, and the women married into one another's families.

Some of their children would have five toes and six toes and one of them had one big eye right in the middle of the forehead, he did—yeah, that's right! Finally the father died, and they decided they wasn't gonna take him to the funeral home and have him embalmed. They was gonna keep him and take him from house to house and keep him forever. So the authorities heard about it and came and told them they had to bury him, had to do something with him.

Well, they all got mad and went to fighting between themselves, the family did. While they was fighting, some of his sons came and grabbed him and stole him and took him off. One of the sons had electricity, and he bought an old deep freeze. When he bought that old deep freeze, they took the dead man and hid him there in order to keep him. It was a year later in the summer when they caught them, and the father was still frozen in the deep freeze. He still looked like he did the day he died, and this was a true story.

This was when electricity came in Eastern Kentucky, back in 1944, and this was when they had State Patrols in the white and blue cars, yeah. I know because my uncle was a policeman.

*Male, age 58, Franklin County*

## Corpse Comes Alive

There was these two guys sittin' up with a dead person. Got way up in the night, and they got hungry. So they had some potatoes, and they decided to roast 'em in the ashes. Back at that time they didn't embalm anybody. A lot of times people was known to be in a trance. They even buried people that way, and they was dug up or opened up later, and they'd turned over in the grave because they was not dead. They had been in a trance.

So these two guys was sittin' up with this corpse. And this guy, they thought he was dead, but he was in a trance. They roasted these potatoes. So, they're down in front of the fireplace. One of them was sayin' "Here's one potato for you and one for me. One for you. One for me."

The guy that was layin' on the cooling board come to. He raised up and said, "Where's *my* potatoes?" He got 'em all, 'cause they went through the window!

*Male, age 59, Scott County*

## Corpse Sits Up

This is a story that happened back when. Do you remember when they used to lay a dead man's body in the home?

*Interviewer: Yes.*

He said his uncle died, and he and his other uncle were sitting up, you know, by the fireplace. Back there on the bed was the dead man, laid out. He said they didn't do anything at all to the body. He said they were sitting there talking, and all at once they glanced around and the body was sitting up in the bed, just straight up in the bed, and after a while he flailed one arm, flailed the other arm. By that time it looked like he was going to get up, you know; he rocked. Both men ran out the door, and one of them hit some pots that hung over the porch, and they caught him by the collar. He thought he was gone; he thought that dead man had done got him.

*Interviewer: He was scared, huh?*

Yes, and his little boy couldn't go to bed at night he was so scared.

*Female, age 65, Scott County*

## Ghost or No Ghost

The only story I could tell isn't really a ghost story, but it could very well pass as one. There was a house built in my hometown of Mertonsville, Kentucky, when I was a boy. The kids that lived in this new house used to talk about it being haunted. Soon the story was all over town about the noise that sounded like a wail that could be heard in this house. People began to talk, and the family decided to try and find what the noise really was.

After years of wondering, they finally realized where the noise was coming from. They cut into the wall and found an old two-handed saw that was still buried in a beam. This saw used to catch the slightest draft and wiggle, making the wailing and banging sound. It sure caused a lot of stories. I guess that's the way most of these stories end up though, isn't it?

*Male, age 40, Scott County*

## Ghost with Chains

Over on the back of the farm that we owned in a holler, there was a mostly log house, and these people moved into it in the spring. It was said that the house had ghosts in it, and that there would be chains that would be drug over the upper floor. Men would go back there, and they could hear it and everything.

One night, they discovered someone's pet coon had gotten loose with a collar and a chain on it, and that the coon was jumping out of a tree onto the back porch and going in a window. He was dragging that chain across the floor. And that's all we can make out of that story.

*Male, age 65, Scott County*

## Churchyard Ghost

There is an old church downtown that has a large churchyard beside
it. It borders the sidewalk for a good distance and is fairly deep. It
backs up to a farm. One time a person was passing by there as it was
getting dark, and he saw a white object that floated up at the back
of the churchyard near some tombstones and then moved down. He
stopped and watched, and, sure enough, he saw it rise up and then
disappear.

The story got around, and soon there were others who saw the
white form hovering and sometimes moving side to side. People who
passed by at night began to cross the street rather than walk close to
the churchyard.

Two boys, about ten and twelve, decided they wanted to see
what the ghost looked like. They hid themselves behind a large monument, not very far from where the ghost usually appeared. It was
a moonlit night. The boys waited, and finally a small bit of white
appeared and then grew larger. It began to bob up and down! When
the boys were able to focus on it, they discovered that it was a white-
faced heifer sticking her head through a hole in the fence to eat the
grass on the other side!

*Male, age 33, Owen County*

## Ghost That Wasn't

Mr. F. T. used to be the superintendent of the cemetery out here,
but he's dead now. Many years ago, he called me one morning when
I was director of admissions at the college and said he had something
he wanted to tell me.

He said he had some men not far from the north gate, and
they were digging a grave. In the afternoon (this was Halloween
time, now) there was what they thought was a woman, and it came
through the north gate riding a broom. It had a witch outfit on, a big
hat, and it was carrying a straw suitcase. It sure scared these men.

What actually happened, Mr. T. said to me, was that some sorority girls from the college were initiating, and their assignment was to walk through that gate in the afternoon, ride the broom, and come on out. These men digging the grave saw her, and as soon as she left, they ran for Mr. T.'s house, which is in the cemetery. These men crowded around Mr. T., and they said, "We've worked for you a long time, and we like you, but if anything like this happens again, we're quitting."

*Male, age 71, Scott County*

## The Corpse That Moved

P.J., he's dead now, but I heard them tell it that when he was a boy, a friend of his died. So back then they laid them on a cooling board, you know, and spread a sheet over them.

This was a little, small house, and the people slept upstairs. So P.J. and this nineteen-year-old boy was gonna sit up with the corpse that night. Way up in the night, P.J. and this boy was talkin', and P.J. said, "Boy, I'm thirsty."

The other boy said, "I am, too."

P.J. said, "What about you going to get some water?"

He said, "Shoot, no!"

P.J. said, "Well, I'll go get some."

He said, "Uh uh. I ain't gonna stay here by myself."

So P.J. said, "Well, you go on and get the bucket of water, and I'll stay here."

So the boy goes out, takes his bucket, and goes to the spring. He had to go around the house by this big rock chimney, a fireplace, you know? He went down a path to the spring. P.J. thought how funny it would be to take the corpse out and stand him in the corner by this stone chimney. And so he did. He took him out and stood him up, then lit a cigar and put it in this dead person's mouth. And there he was. Of course, he's stiff as a board. Standing there, way up in the night, and this cigar was lit, which made a light.

This boy come back. He's carryin' this bucket. When he walked around, he looked up and there stood the corpse, smoking a cigar. They said that guy screamed and throwed that bucket and took off! He lived about a mile and a half through the country. They said when the boy got home he'd torn almost all of his clothes off. He was cut all to pieces. He'd run through a barbed wire fence and everything, and run right through the door when he got home!

Well, P.J., he just picks the corpse up and throws the cigar away, and brings the corpse back in, lays it down, and spreads the sheet back over it. The people heard the boy scream, so they run downstairs to see what had happened. And P.J. is standing at the door looking out. They said, "What happened?"

P.J. said, "I don't know. I heard that boy scream." So they all go out and look, and they can't find him. The parents, they come to see what had happened, but they couldn't prove it on P.J. If they could of, they would like to have sent him to the penitentiary. It didn't come out till years and years later that he did a trick like that. And he admitted it then.

*Male, age 59, Scott County*

## Dead Man Speaks

A man died and was to be buried in the local cemetery. It happened that the grave digger knew the man who died personally. The body was laying topside while the grave digger was in the hole digging out the grave. Another man came looking for him, and he called the grave digger by name. Upon hearing his name, he thought the dead man was calling him. He jumped out of that grave and took off running!

*Male, age 65, Scott County*

## False Belief in Ghosts

This is a sad story. It happened in Hawesville, Indiana. My brother lived in a big old house. It's hard telling how old it was. It had been a captain's house.

The house had three stories. Of a night in winter, the stove door would open up, and the house would get hot. The stair-steps door would be open. My brother was kind of scared of the house, but they couldn't find another house to live in. So he nailed the door shut.

Every night the door would come open. The board would come unnailed and be laying on the floor. The fire would be hot, and, in the kitchen, there would always be some pots and pans scattered around.

We went to visit, and he showed me upstairs where there were lots of old pictures and furniture and antiques. He told me about the ghost.

That night we could hear noises, and steps on the stairs. We looked, and, sure enough, the stair-door was open again! I kind of thought it was my brother doing it, so my wife and I laughed it off and went back to bed.

About three or four months later my brother moved. One afternoon after he'd moved out, the house caught on fire. The fire department came, and they kept hearing screaming and yelling. My brother and some of them were saying that they kept telling people the place was haunted.

They couldn't put out the fire. After it burned itself out, they started looking to see what caused the fire. They found that there was this orphan boy who had been living in the crawl space of the basement.

He had been going up in the house at night building up the fire, and going upstairs to sleep. You know it's rather tragic. In this case, it was believing in ghosts rather than the reality that there might be somebody living in the house that caused his death. They might have saved his life if they'd known it.

*Male, age mid-30s, Henry County*

## UFO or Ghost?

This one particular incident happened about, oh, say, six years ago. I was building a house right on the Scott-Franklin County line, just off Cedar Road. There wasn't any electricity up there, so my wife and I would go up there and work till it got dark. Then we'd have to quit at dark. This one particular night, we quit right at dark and started home. We came in from Stamping Ground and turned right there at the grocery and went across Wilson's at Ironworks, then turned left. The radio station is right there.

I turned left on Ironworks Pike, and I hadn't gone maybe three hundred feet. I was driving a green pickup truck, a real dark green pickup truck. We got halfway between the house on the left and the radio station on the right. I looked up, and there was a light coming across that field on the left-hand side of the road. The light kept getting bigger and bigger and bigger. I told my wife, "That's odd that a plane would have its landing lights on."

When the light came up close, I come to a stop. The light was just off to our left in the middle of the field, looked like a hundred, maybe two hundred, feet off the ground. Pretty soon it had the whole field lit up. It had the road lit up, the field lit up.

My wife said, "Look! Look! The truck, it's blue!" I looked at our truck. The truck looked blue. In that light, I swear, that light, it changed the color in my eyes. It didn't change the paint. It just made it look blue. I looked back and the whole field was lit up bright. The light got up even with me and suddenly it made a ninety-degree right turn and went . . . swoosh! It didn't take it to the count of four: one, two, three, four, and it was out of sight!

*Male, age 52, Scott County*

## Self-Fulfilling Prophecy

As I recall, my grandmother told me a story that really happened. It isn't a ghost story or anything like that, but it is a weird story.

The townspeople were building a new courthouse, and the intended site for the building was going to be over a grave. There was some controversy over the building, but everybody more or less agreed that it should be built there, grave or no grave.

There was this old man who greatly opposed the building of the courthouse over the grave. And one afternoon, just prior to the time when the building was supposed to be begun, he said, "I hope I never live to see the day when that building is built!" Sure enough, the next morning he woke up blind! And the townspeople built their building!

*Male, age 23, Woodford County*

# Notes

1. Jan Bondeson, *Buried Alive: The Terrifying History of Our Most Primal Fear* (New York: W. W. Norton, 2001), 125.

*Chapter 8*

# Ghosts at Educational Institutions

At most older colleges and universities ghost stories have been passed down through generations of students. Stories are spreading at newer schools as well, as life—and death—go on. A well-known ritual involves upperclassmen acquainting new students, especially the most gullible ones, with tales of strange noises, unexplained movements of objects, sightings of shadowy figures, and other evidence of ghosts that have been seen on campus. This is also true in boarding schools, where the students, being younger, are even more impressionable.

As ghost stories are repeated, slight alterations are made. Often it is interesting to compare versions of the same story related by different individuals. The basic facts will be the same, but the details may be embellished or changed altogether. This can be seen in the versions of "The Kappa Delta Ghost" (at Georgetown College), which are here related by several different persons, who provide different interpretations of the ghostly young woman's identity and background.

One reason that schools are such a good source of ghost stories is that where many people are gathered, there is a good chance that the suggestion of a ghost will elicit sympathetic responses from some of them. They will be watching out for evidence, and will be likely to construe an unusual event as proof of a supernatural happening. If one is told that a dorm room is haunted by someone who committed suicide there, one is more apt to notice and be alarmed by any sound that is heard in that vicinity.

Reports of ghosts on campuses seem to have increased in recent years, and this may be partly in response to a greater interest in the paranormal, fostered by the number of television programs portraying such events. Students are now sharing their stories and experiences via e-mail, text messaging, and postings on blogs. At most institutions, people now accept reports of ghostly events as part of their heritage, and don't hesitate to share stories. Some schools, such as Wells College in Aurora, New York,[1] and Franklin and Marshall College in Lancaster, Pennsylvania,[2] have even established Web sites for sharing these stories. (This is certainly a change from sharing ghost stories around a campfire on a dark night!)

Central Kentucky has no shortage of institutions of learning that have famous ghosts as residents. Whether it is the ghost of Dr. Funkhouser visiting with Coach Rupp at the University of Kentucky, or the coed ghost who "moved" to a new dorm when her old one was torn down at Georgetown College, their tales are all part of the lore of many generations of students.

## Governor Robinson's Ghost

Cardome used to be a school for girls. Before that it was Governor Robinson's home. Legend has it that Governor Robinson's ghost could be seen walking down the staircase on one particular night of the year. It was a big thing for the girls to stay up on that night and watch for him.

*Female, age unknown, Scott County*

## Ghost Warded Off

When Governor Robinson lived at Cardome and was getting on in years, it was known that he had gout, and he had to use a cane which had quite a distinctive sound. At Cardome there are two big dormitories. They both come in off the porch, and these girls kept hearing something like someone who walked with a limp on the

Cardome Academy, Georgetown, Kentucky. (Photograph by Tim Anderson, courtesy of Mayor Karen Sames, Georgetown, Kentucky.)

porch. The girls said something to the nuns who replied that it was "Sister somebody."

Well, at the time this took place, "Sister whoever" was bed-ridden, so it couldn't have been her. Anyway they kept hearing the walking at night and also a child crying, and the girls kept saying something about it, and they were told to just forget it. There was nothing to it.

But there was one girl—I believe her name was Diane—who was a very down-to-earth child, nothing flighty about her at all. Well, one night they heard footsteps on the floor, then the screen door (which had quite a screech to it) open and close. This one child, Diane, stuck her head out to see what was going on, and it walked right past her down the hall to another door, which she saw open and close! All the girls took a dim view of that!

So Diane waited a little bit, and of course all Catholic schools and dormitories have holy water and a crucifix in the room. So she made up her mind that if "that" came back toward them, she would get the crucifix down off the wall. So in a few minutes the door opened and closed. Then she said she just backed into the dormitory and got the crucifix down and a little holy water, and she just waited. So when "it" came toward her, she put the holy water and the crucifix in front of it, and the girls say the door stopped opening and the crying child was never heard again.

*Female, age unknown, Madison County*

## Piano-Playing Ghost

You know of Cardome? Well, there was a group of girls, including my daughter Katie, who was a day student at the time. Have you ever been in Cardome? There is an older part where there were practice rooms downstairs, and there was an old stairway. This house used to belong to the former Governor Robinson.

Down at the bottom of the stairway and to the right were the practice rooms for the piano students. One practice room was apparently, from the way they figured it, a part of the original drawing room or music room. One time the girls kept hearing music coming from the practice room, and, being girls, they decided they wanted to see what was going on.

So they toddled downstairs, and they swore and declared that they saw this woman who was dressed in a white dress certainly not of this period, but one of many, many years ago. It was low cut, white, and she was blond and very beautiful, and she played this same song over and over and over again. Well, the nuns heard it themselves, and when the other ghost stories came along, the nuns hushed it up.

*Female, age unknown, Madison County*

## Coed Returns to Transylvania

A pretty, blonde Transylvania College student was found murdered in her car, which was parked on the circle in front of Morrison Hall. She had been strangled with her own bra. Despite investigations, her killer was never identified.

Over the years, residents of Forrer Hall, the women's dorm on Transylvania's campus, reported glimpsing a transparent, tall, thin blonde figure in the dorm or walking across campus. Some years after the murder, a Forrer Hall resident awoke one night and saw a young woman bent over, rummaging through her dresser drawer. Before she could speak, the apparition disappeared!

Shortly after this, some students were gathered around a Ouija board asking questions. They knew of this incident and claim to have used the board to talk to the ghost and ask her why she was rummaging in the drawer. The response they got so unnerved them that they left their dorm and went to the student center where there were more people.

It seems that when they asked the ghost why she had been in the room in Forrer Hall, she replied that a friend had taken her purse and there was a letter in it from her boyfriend which she had not read. When asked who had taken her purse, she said "Carol" and a last name which was not clear on the Ouija board, but which started with a "D."

Several of us went to the library the next day and looked in old yearbooks. We found photos of a young woman who had the first name of Carol and whose last name began with a "D." The amazing thing was that she looked very much like the girl who had seen the ghost going through her drawers, and she was in school at the same time as the young student who had been killed!

This ghost is still seen on the Transylvania campus. According to some, she has been seen walking through a wall of Forrer Hall that has been added since she was a student there. She is still being glimpsed, conspicuous by her 1960s attire, particularly in the vicinity of the driveway in front of Old Morrison.

*Female, age 40, Fayette County*

## Apparitions in Old Giddings

In the basement, before Giddings Hall was restored, the theater people used to have a storeroom. They always had a problem with it.

After it was closed up and locked, shoes would disappear, just one of them, one of a pair would disappear. So it would be gone a day or two, and all of a sudden it would be returned!

One of the biggest stories that happened in Giddings was in 1969. College security had to visit each floor of Giddings on their rounds. Well, these two guys went up to the third floor. They went in the lobby, and, as they walked by, there was a light coming from under the doors of another storage room.

So they decided they'd go in and check it. They went to open the door, and the light disappeared! OK, so now that the light's off in there, they opened it up, went in, and, with flashlights and billy clubs, walked around and took a look, and there's nothing there.

It's that big third floor where they've got a conference room now. They just walked clear across it and came back, so when they're about halfway back, all of a sudden there's a light in back of them. They turn around, and they see this really strange thing, you know, like some kind of little lights, and something sort of weird, sort of a cloud, suspended in the air. So they tore the hell out of there, and went back and locked themselves in the security room. The next morning both of them resigned; they wouldn't put up with that mess.

*Male, age 20, Scott County*

*The above story as well as the following two are some of several stories collected from various parties concerning Giddings Hall, Georgetown College's first permanent structure. Built by students and faculty in 1841, the building has had many uses over the years, having housed the sciences departments and the theater prior to its current use as an administration building.*

# Child Returns

Someone told about a ghost in Giddings Hall. One of the security guards was on the second floor making his rounds. When he turned around, he saw this little girl dressed in ruffles standing by the door at the end of the hall. He thought at first it was a kid who'd hidden in the building. He knew that kids had hidden in the building before

Giddings Hall, Georgetown College, Georgetown, Kentucky. (Photograph by Tim Anderson, courtesy of Georgetown College.)

when it was being locked up, and he was afraid that they'd broken into the offices. He stopped and checked the president's office, then crossed over to check the Development Office door.

He looked away just a second, and when he looked back, she was gone. "Someone must have left those rear doors unlocked," he thought. He walked down to the doors and tested them, but they were locked. There was no other way she could have gone, and no way she could get past him. When this sank in, he felt suddenly terrified and left in a hurry!

When he told this, one of the older faculty members said he knew about this ghost. When Giddings was being built in the late 1830s, a little girl from the neighborhood used to come over and play in the building.

One day, as she often did, she left some toys in the building when she went home. That night she came down with a heavy fever and died. Some time later people began seeing her in Giddings. They said she is looking for her toys.

*Male, age unknown, Scott County*

## Giddings Hall Phantom

Before Giddings Hall was remodeled, students used to go there to be
alone. One night this couple went there, and they heard a typewriter
going. They went upstairs, thinking it was someone working late.
They thought they should investigate it. They found the place where
the sound was coming from. They opened the door, and there was
a small, white figure like the shape of a little girl. The figure chased
them down the steps. They decided they shouldn't have been run off
and they were going back upstairs. They went back up to see the girl.
Now, there was only one way up there, but when they got upstairs
she wasn't there, and she hadn't come down those stairs!

*Male, age 20, Scott County*

## Rucker Hall Ghost

At one time the main women's dormitory on the Georgetown College campus was a large brick structure named Rucker Hall, built in
the late nineteenth century. There was one room on the fourth floor
that was kept locked for many years. Several generations of coeds
claimed that the room was haunted. It is said that in the early part
of the twentieth century, a young lady was taken advantage of by
a male student who jilted her. She was heartbroken and eventually
hung herself in her room in Rucker Hall.

A few girls claim to have seen her as a shape or to have felt her
presence. Anyone who tried to live there moved out. They said it just
felt awful in there. And on some occasions when girls were assigned
that room, they seldom stayed in it for long.

*Female, age 60, Scott County*

*The above story as well as the following two stories all refer to the
same ghost, who, when its residence was demolished, began to appear in a new building that was constructed over a portion of the
site where its previous home had stood.*

Rucker Hall, Georgetown College, Georgetown, Kentucky. The ghost of the jilted coed may be looking out the middle window on the third floor. (Courtesy of the archives at Georgetown College, Georgetown, Kentucky.)

## Ghost Changes Residences

There is a ghost in the Phi Mu House. One corner of the Phi Mu House is built over Rucker Hall. Rucker Hall was demolished in the late 1960s, you know. It's over a room where a girl hung herself in her closet, because she had been jilted. Anyway, in the third floor corner room, in the back, which is the only corner of the Phi Mu House that is over where Rucker used to be, people hear pounding on the walls, and it gets a lot colder in that room. Like one night, somebody heard it pounding clear down on the second floor. —— was living on the second floor and she heard it, all the way down on the second floor.

*Female, age 20, Scott County*

## Sorority Ghost

There is a ghost in the Phi Mu house. I think it is the one from

Phi Mu Sorority House, Georgetown College, Georgetown, Kentucky.
(Photograph by Tim Anderson, courtesy of Georgetown College.)

Rucker Hall, or maybe it's the Kappa Delta ghost, I'm not sure. The
ghost is always making noises and doing strange things. Sometimes
it scares the girls to death. You can especially hear it in ——'s room
'cause that's where the girl supposedly hung herself. All I know is
that it stomps around making all kinds of noises.

*Female, age 18, Scott County*

## Kappa Delta Resident Relates Experience

I am telling this story because it has affected me and some of my
sister Kappa Deltas at Georgetown College.

I moved into the KD house the second semester of my freshman
year. The house is old, maybe going back to the mid-1870s. It has a
large hall at the front, and the stairs to the second floor ascend from
this entry. It makes an impressive picture when one descends the
steps to greet a visitor.

Most of the sorority sisters live on the second floor, though not
all. There are two areas in particular on the second floor, and one

on the first floor, that I think hold the spirit of a young woman from Puerto Rico who lived in the house as an indentured servant.

Often, people entertaining guests in the drawing room on the left side of the entryway will hear someone walking up the steps or scraping the woodwork on the staircase. When they go to look, there is nobody there, although once or twice a pan with soapy water has been found. Sometimes, they will hear footsteps going up the stairs to the top, where they stop! I have heard these footsteps myself. On the second floor there are sometimes lighthearted comments about the KD ghost. I know a couple of girls who believe in the ghost because of encounters they have had with her.

As for me, it was well into February before my first experience with the KD ghost occurred. I had a fleeting glimpse of a younger teenage girl on the landing of the stairs. I was engrossed in cramming for a test when I decided to go to the bathroom, which was at the back of the second floor. I barely nodded to her and marched past on my bathroom trip. It struck me that she was younger, but she could have been visiting. Then I thought, in the middle of the week?

My second encounter was also late at night. I stepped out of our room, readying myself for bed. I noticed a teenaged girl with black hair standing close to one of the doors. I nodded and traveled on to the lavatory. When I emerged a few minutes later, the young lady was looking over the railing that went around the staircase. I spoke to her. She stared at me balefully. As I approached, she disappeared!

I have grown accustomed to seeing the spirit occasionally, or hearing her march up the steps from the first floor. It seems a pity that she cannot be released and be able to get some peace.

*Female, age 19, Fayette County*

*From our research we have selected four variations of the story of the Kappa Delta (KD) ghost, which was also mentioned above in "Sorority Ghost." Version one is the above story, and versions two through four are the following three stories. This was a very popular story on the Georgetown College campus and was passed on to each new generation of students, especially Kappa Delta sorority members. Stories such as this become varied as they are retold, thus there is some disagreement about whether the spirit was a student or a servant. Three of the stories are accounts of personal experiences with the ghost, related by young persons who lived in the house. The fourth is a more objective account given by a longtime professor well versed in the history of the college.*

## Family's Experience in Former KD House

The college eventually moved the KDs to the residence area of the main campus where Rucker Hall used to be. Not all KD alums knew about this, and for about four months after we moved in, people would walk in and head upstairs. They did not realize that the house was now our home, since our dad was director of development for the college, and the house was one of his benefits.

Once things settled down, we began to notice strange happenings. Our family gathered in the lounge, one of the KD parlors, to watch the national and local news, and then we would hear the front door open and footsteps go up the stairs. The difference was now we tried to keep the door latched at all times. So, someone was asked to see who had come in. It got to be a thing, you know. Door is locked, someone walks across the entry and upstairs, but there isn't anyone there!

Lights will sometimes come on upstairs or in the entryway in the evening. Now that there are no visitors and it's just us, we can do a quick roll call and know that the one making noise in the upstairs, or turning on lights, is *not* one of us.

*Male, age 21, Scott County*

## The Kappa Delta Ghost

As far as I know, the Kappa Delta house at Georgetown College was built before the Civil War, and in the basement, it's supposed to have a trapdoor that leads to a well outside. The trapdoor is now covered with a big concrete pillar. Sometime between 1920 and 1940, I believe, there was a girl who hung herself from our chandelier. We have a winding staircase and there was a humongous chandelier in the entrance hall. They moved it, I believe, to Dr. Mill's home.

From what I know, she climbed on top of the spindle at the bottom of the staircase, tied a rope to the chandelier, and when somebody came down the next morning, they saw feet swinging. I don't know when the ghost story started. When we moved in, all of the KDs kept coming over and saying, "Have you heard anything about the ghost?" and we would say, "What ghost?"

Now, we didn't hear anything for six or seven months after we moved in. I remember when we first moved after the house had just been painted. I kept seeing these little red spots all over the place—on tops of doors, on window sills, and in stupid places. It looked like someone had taken a toothbrush, just dipped it and splattered it. The house was not painted red anywhere. The house was just painted white on white.

The day we moved in, they were still painting. They got through, and the spots started turning up everywhere. On the staircase you can still see them. They are all over the place. I can't tell if they are fresh or old. I said to myself right after we moved in that the house had just been painted, and that's stupid.

As I said, six or seven months after we moved in, we started hearing things. It would just be a little bit at first, a clunk upstairs, made you think something had fallen off a table or something like that. But late one night we heard something on the stairs. It sounded like somebody walking on the stairs. Thinking maybe someone was sick, we turned on the lights, and there was nobody on the stairs. We went back to bed, and something started clunking on the stairs again. I didn't hear anything until a little bit after that.

I remember my brother and I were in my room one night, and we heard what sounded like scratching on the ceiling. We have fifteen foot ceilings, and that leaves about three and a half feet in the attic, so no one can stand up. I thought it was a squirrel, so I started throwing things up and tapping on the ceiling to make it run around.

Whatever it was—I'll call it "it"—stood there, like, fifteen minutes, and then I heard something start to walk. This sounds corny and dumb, but you can tell the difference between something just walking and something walking with army boots. You could hear a clunk and a creaking of the boards. If it was a squirrel or a bat— we've got a lot of bats—you could tell because there's nothing about a bat to make that kind of noise or clunk like that.

It was scary then, but sometimes, once a month, you could hear "it" coming, in the room that is supposed to be haunted at the top of the stairs. You could hear "it" walk all over the room, stand a second, make some noise, then walk over to the bathroom. It would go from room to room, but not any more in the haunted room than anywhere else. It can happen upstairs in any room.

There is an old KD tale that some girl left a dress in a chair, and she was talking to her friend. She said there was a little girl wearing the dress when she turned around. She screamed and ran out. When she came back in, the dress was in the chair.

I know I still hear stuff. It freaks us out. It's really cool.

*Male, age 22, Scott County*

*Although not mentioned in this story, the informant told us that plaster falls from the ceiling in the spot where the footsteps are heard, he and his family feel cold bursts of air when there are no doors or windows open, and their two dogs run up to a particular room barking and acting scared.*

## History of KD Ghost by Georgetown Professor

The fine old home, Estillhurst, has been associated with Georgetown College for many years. In the nineteenth century, the college purchased the building to house students of the Female Seminary. Later, the building was the home of the ladies of the Kappa Delta sorority.

It is not known if the spirit who became known as the KD ghost was a servant or a student at the seminary. What is known is that the ghost has been experienced by many generations of KDs.

The stories, as related by residents, are similar—seeing a "stranger" on the second floor, hearing the front door open and shut after curfew even though the door was bolted shut from the inside, and hearing footsteps going up the grand staircase but no one appearing on the landing.

Encounters with the spirit have been numerous. Most relate seeing a young girl dressed in white who then disappears in front of their eyes. It is also apparent that the spirit wished no harm to anyone.

One local legend has it that a young seminary student had become depressed. She ultimately carried material up the steps with which she fashioned a noose that she tied to the chandelier. She placed her head in the noose, climbed up onto the stair railing, and then stepped off into space. It seems, from reports of recent residents of the house, that the young lady still lives there.

*Male, age 50, Scott County*

## Scholar Reappears

Before Dr. Funkhouser died, he taught several classes at the university, and he was a scientist. He wrote several things on ghosts and was preoccupied with spirits.

Now he hides things from me, and when my sister and her children lived here with me, she said she couldn't sleep. She said she loved the house, but she can't stand to live here. Nobody with children could live in this house from the time it was built. Later I rented it to a couple with children while I lived on Broadway. They were robbed twelve times. Nobody has robbed me, and I've lived here ten years. Sometimes the door would open at night and nobody was there. This still happens. But he wanted to get rid of them all, and he did, and I never rented to families with children again.

I saw Mr. Funkhouser once when I was digging up his garden. I came back toward the house, and I saw someone. I had a boy renting with me at that time. I thought for a minute it was the boy, but then I thought he was too old for Bill. It was just a glance. I came into the kitchen door, and I kept calling, "Bill," but there was no Bill there!

I took his swing down one night, and Funkhouser looked for the swing all night! He went up in the attic; he went everyplace. The boy living with me at that time was a graduate of Yale and a real

cynic. He asked me what I had been doing in the attic the night before, and I said it was Funkhouser looking for his swing.

The strangest thing that happened was after I moved back here.
I had a man sanding my floors. It was a Sunday afternoon, really
late. He said he was going to go on and sand until he got tired, which
could be around 9 or 10 p.m. He said, "Don't be worried if you see
lights on."

So I said OK and that I was going on.

The next morning I came back, and he said, "I thought you left
last night."

I said, "I did leave; why?"

He said, "You couldn't have left; there was somebody upstairs
moving furniture all night."

I said, "Well, I guess it was Funkhouser."

He likes to stay in the front room upstairs. That's his favorite
room, and nobody can stay there. I had a girl who tried to stay there
one time, and she complained that she couldn't sleep. She said, "I
guess I was dreaming. It was just like someone waving a sheet over
my head, and, as you would say, a ghost swishing back and forth." I
had another one, a boy up there, that told me the same thing.

Funkhouser hated cats, and one day the girl came in with two
cats. She kept them upstairs in that bedroom, and they were shiver-
ing and shaking, scared to death. She brought them here on Saturday
morning, and by Monday morning she said, "They can't stay up
there; they're scared to death."

Mr. Funkhouser picks out my tenants. If he doesn't like them, he
makes sure they don't stay long. I had one boy who heard a tapping
all night long, and finally it felt like something was tapping on his
head. He left to go somewhere else where he could get some sleep.

My sister with the children said she kept hearing doors open
and close all night long, and she couldn't sleep. She says she doesn't
believe in ghosts, but she would ask the strangest things, like, "Why
don't you answer the door? Someone's knocking," and no one would
be there. She has a great capacity for hearing things or sensing that
someone is there.

Dr. ——, a psychologist, came to my house and was putting his coat in the closet. He came back in and asked who my tenant was. I said I didn't have a tenant at the time. He said, "Whose coat is that in the closet?" I said I didn't know. Then he said it was a man's coat, and I said it must be Dr. Funkhouser's.

I feel his presence all the time. When I feel lonely, I know he's gone. And even when I'm alone, I don't feel like I'm by myself. I know he's here.

One morning about 11:30 a woman and her son came to look at the house. I had a boy boarding here at the time, and he was watching while I took them from room to room. After they left, the boy asked me who the other old woman with me was. I said there was no one with me, just the woman and her son. He went on to describe the lady, and it fit the description of Mrs. Funkhouser that I had gotten from the neighbors.

I had a dog one time that wouldn't go into the entrance hall. If he wanted to go to the living room from here, he would walk through the kitchen and all the way around through the back of the house. He would never go upstairs, and once, when somebody carried him upstairs, he quivered and shook and ran back down. One day the dog went in the living room and sat down beside a chair. There wasn't anybody there, but he was acting exactly as he did when someone was petting him.

Before he died, Dr. Funkhouser told a neighbor that he would never leave this house, and then, after his death, the bank sold the house at an auction because Mrs. Funkhouser was really incapable. The night they decided to auction it off, the nurse staying with Mrs. Funkhouser went to the neighbors across the street about four in the morning. She said Dr. Funkhouser was tearing the house up, stamping up and down the steps, and raising hell! She still refuses to step foot in this house. But Dr. Funkhouser is more or less a feeling to me. Other people have seen him in the house, but not me. I don't want to.

I also have a picture of Dr. Funkhouser. One of my tenants was taking a picture of my corner cupboard, and, when we looked at it, we saw Funkhouser was standing in front of the French doors! It's a Polaroid picture, and it is not a reflection of the man taking the pictures. The man in the picture had on a long coat about to his knees, and the sleeves hung very long. He had on a string tie. You can't make out any bodily features. There is a very light trace of the head, but it can't be seen clearly. The picture is about twelve years old. There is also a large blob of light next to where his head should have been. It's his aura, where the spirit is.

Funkhouser was a big sports fan, and he died in 1948. I think the [University of Kentucky] coliseum was dedicated in 1949. I don't remember the year for sure, but he died the year before the building was dedicated. Adolph Rupp said that Funkhouser was with him when they opened it and when they closed it. He mentioned it in three or four articles in the different papers, that "I think Funkhouser was with me." On occasion, Rupp would say he'd been in his office with Funkhouser.

*Female, age 60, Fayette County*

*Often a strong-willed person will exert his or her presence in a residence or place of work. This seems to be the case with the well-known University of Kentucky scholar Dr. William D. Funkhouser (1881–1948), who served as chairman of the Zoology Department and dean of graduate studies, and who manifests both at his long-time home and at the university on occasion. A building on the University of Kentucky campus is named for him.*

## An Eerie Evening

—— was working security one night and was up on the third floor of Giddings Hall at Georgetown College where they have those big old dark rooms. He heard some footsteps or someone walking around up on the third floor. He and another boy went up there and looked all around and didn't see anybody, but it is probably pretty easy to hide. As they were walking back out the door to go down to the second floor, they heard a thud next to their heads. They looked up

John L. Hill Chapel, Georgetown College, Georgetown, Kentucky. (Photograph by Tim Anderson, courtesy of Georgetown College.)

on the door frame, and there was this knife sticking in the side of the door.

They trucked on down. It was one of those spring nights, really foggy; you could hardly see anything. It was so bad you couldn't see from one streetlight to the next. They went on out and were walking back up to the chapel. About this time, they looked up and there was this light getting closer and closer and closer. All of a sudden, it flashed real bright like a flashbulb going off, and then disappeared! They got on the walkie-talkie and talked to someone on the other part of campus and asked if he had seen a flash of light, but of course he hadn't.

*Male, age 20, Scott County*

## Mysterious Light on the Chapel

This was told to me by a buddy who works for security. He and this other security guy were coming up the south campus toward the [John L. Hill] Chapel. It was late, about 2 a.m.

They were going back toward the chapel when they saw this light that glowed all around the edges of the steeple. It was like the Northern Lights. It lasted a couple of seconds, and they both saw it.

Next day, it was announced that the guy the chapel is named for had died in the night.

*Male, age 20, Scott County*

## Notes

1. Wells College, "From the Archives—Ghost Stories Told by Students," *Wells College Library,* http://aurora.wells.edu/~library/ghosts.htm (accessed December 17, 2008).

2. Franklin and Marshall College, "F&M Ghost Stories," *Archives and Special Collections at F&M College Library,* http://library.fandm.edu/archives/ghoststories.html (accessed December 17, 2008).

*Chapter 9*

# Death Omens and Superstitions

"See a pin; pick it up; all the day you'll have good luck." "Don't step on a crack or you'll break your mother's back." "If you find a penny with its head up, you will have good luck."

Superstitions? Probably. Real predictions of things to come? Surely not! Yet even those who scoff at such sayings may find themselves picking up pins and avoiding cracks in the sidewalk. Most of us feel uncomfortable walking under ladders. People still regard Friday the thirteenth as—potentially—a bad luck day. Some athletes will wear the same socks or other item of clothing as good luck, and the lucky articles will not be washed as long as the athlete is winning. One could go on and on recounting superstitious beliefs, which are numerous and varied.

Death omens are common to all cultures. For example, the clicking sound of the deathwatch beetle foreshadows death in a family according to many people in England, the United States, and parts of Europe.[1] The omens of death are numerous and varied. The appearance of a bird in one's house means a death in the family, and certain birds such as crows or owls can foretell a death. The howling of a dog, or the appearance of a ghostly coach, or the sound of its wheels trundling outside can frighten a family, particularly if one member is ill.

Death omens abound in literature. Shakespeare uses omens to foretell death in many of his plays. One omen he uses in *Anthony and Cleopatra* was an eclipse of the moon to predict the death of Mark Anthony. In *The Raven,* Edgar Allan Poe uses a sinister black bird that will not leave the perch above the narrator's door as an omen of his own death to come.

One could go on and on recounting superstitious beliefs and omens. This chapter contains several stories of death omens and beliefs about death collected from Central Kentuckians. We think you'll find them interesting. (Knock on wood!)

## Apparition Foretells Death

When I was little, my grandmother used to tell the story about when her little boy, Charlie, was at the point of death. They were quarantined in with typhoid fever, and the doctor had told them that Charlie would never make it, that he would die. So her and Grandpa had set up with him night and day, and they were tired, so when they got the little boy to sleep that night, they went out on the porch, and was setting there just resting.

All at once they looked up, and they saw something come to the fence. It looked like it was a white figure with outstretched hands. So they sat there awhile, and they looked at it, and wondered what it was. Then all at once, Grandpa got up, and as he walked near the fence, it just disappeared.

Grandma said that was an omen that her little boy was going to die, and, sure enough, late that same night, he died.

*Female, age 51, Harrison County*

## Clock Strikes Before Death

My mother told me that one night before Grandpa got killed, she was sitting in their living room late, finishing sewing a dress. They had a clock in the bedroom that hadn't run for years, but at twelve o'clock that night, the clock struck.

She said it wasn't long after that someone knocked on their door and told them that Grandpa had got killed at Lair Station on the railroad at twelve o'clock, the same time Mama had heard the clock strike. After that night, the clock never struck again.

*Female, age 69, Harrison County*

## Muted Noise Precedes Death

My half-Indian grandmother told me this one time. I was staying with my grandparents in their house when I was about nine years old, but I was too young to understand what was happening at the time. My grandmother claimed to have heard some sort of muted noise prior to my grandfather's death. This noise would come and go. All of a sudden it ceased about the time my grandfather passed away. She and I were the only ones present when he died. She didn't know that he was that close to death.

*Male, age 50, Harrison County*

## Black Christmas

If there is no snow at Christmas, then many people will die. My mother said, "A black Christmas, a fat graveyard."

*Female, age 60, Scott County*

*Such unseasonable weather is also called a "green winter," which refers to an unusually warm year with little or no snow, when it doesn't get cold enough to kill germs and vermin.*

## The Devil Can't Cross Water

If the devil came after you, the only way to get away from him was to cross water.

*Female, age 50, Scott County*

## Burning Hair Causes Death

Our mother never would let us comb our hair and put the combings from the hair on the fire. It was bad luck, and you were going to die.

*Female, age 60, Scott County*

## Premonition of Death

My younger brother, Johnny, was always a favorite of my grandmother's, and he went to visit her all the time. Well, one night at about two or three o'clock, Johnny was in bed, and a figure of our grandmother appeared and said, "Johnny, don't be afraid, because I love you."

That was all, and Johnny went downstairs and told my parents. They sorta dismissed him because it was so late, and because he had been sleeping. But the next day, he still remembered. The funny thing was, he wasn't scared; he was just worried.

Later that morning the family had a phone call, and it was discovered that grandmother was dead. She had died the night before.

*Female, age 28, Scott County*

## Footsteps Before Death

One week before my daddy died, there were footsteps in the attic. One day my friend —— came in, and he said, "Mary, do you have someone working in the attic?"

"No," I said. "That has been going on for two or three days."

On Saturday, I went over to my neighbor's house for a little while to visit, and when I came home I said, "Daddy, what have you been doing?"

He said, "Mary, I have had the most wonderful talk with your mother. She was so beautiful, and I enjoyed talking to her. It was the best visit we've ever had. She was prettier than I've ever seen her before."

I didn't know what to say to him because my mother was dead, so I dismissed it. The footsteps were still going on in the attic. Then on Monday, my daddy passed away. I then noticed the footsteps had quit, and I never heard them again.

*Male, age 62, Harrison County*

## Family Banshee Foretells Deaths

I'm going to give you the background to the story to help you understand it better. My mother was Rebecca Thompson, and her grandfather, William, came from Ireland in the late 1700s to this country. His father had been a political refugee from England to Ireland and had taken an assumed name, so we do not know his real name, but the name he took was David Thompson. He married Katherine O'Donohue, who was of the line of the Duke of Argyle.

From this family came the banshee. A banshee is a female spirit who forewarns about a person's death. In the case of the one in our family, she did not wail and moan, but the spirit was restless. Neither my sister nor I have seen any manifestations of the banshee. Evidently, after a number of generations this—whatever the spirit is—weakened, or, as a friend of mine who is Irish said, "She has gone back to the bogs of Ireland."

Anyway, William came from Dublin, where he graduated from the University of Dublin or Trinity College. He was a Protestant, not Catholic. He came to Philadelphia and established a school there. The way he happened to come to Kentucky and this area was that he taught Greek, Hebrew, and Latin at Centre around 1835. In the meantime, his wife died, and his small son stayed with people in this area. When William Thompson came from Ireland to this area as a teacher, the banshee came with him.

My grandmother's father owned a farm near Dovers, and it was at this particular place that some of the manifestations of the banshee took place, and my great-aunt wrote about them. There were two things that stood out in my mind from what my great-aunt wrote. They had some walnut logs lying out in the front yard, being seasoned for furniture and such. One moonlit night they could hear these logs being lifted and dropped with great crashes, crashes that you could hear for miles, and yet they stood at the window and not a log moved. Not too long after that, they had word that a cousin had died.

Right before William Thompson's death, the spirit was evidently very restless. The thing that impressed me the most was what happened the Christmas before he died. My great-aunt wrote that she got up very early to catch the housemaid, to give her a Christmas gift. She said she could hear the housemaid coming up the steps, and, as she came up the hall, my great-aunt opened the door, but there wasn't anyone there.

The steps continued down the hall, and she felt the breath of air of the spirit passing, and she heard the rustling of her skirts as she passed on down the hall into the room at the end. She, the spirit, passed right through the door. William Thompson died not too long after this.

*Female, age 50, Woodford County*

*Banshees are said to announce an impending death to a family. They usually appear in stories from Ireland and Scotland, but this banshee apparently followed the family to Kentucky in the New World.*

## Bird as Death Omen

My husband, W., died, and it was foretold before he died by a fortune-teller. This is funny; it sounds crazy. The fortune-teller said that W. would die quickly at the time of year the cherries were just starting to get ripe. Well, I told my husband about what the fortune-teller said. For about a year or two, after the cherries ripened, he would say, "Well, good for another year!" The year he died, he was found dead in some girl's apartment.

Well, the funny part, though, is this bird. I never believed in that ever before. I was living alone. Both my sons were married, and my daughter was away in college. I was separated from my husband, and I was feeling blue. I was in the kitchen, and a bird kept jumping up on my kitchen window and kept peckin' and peckin'. So I went in the living room, and that bird followed me to that window and kept peckin', peckin', peckin'. It was so unusual 'cause it was night and day. It nearly drove me crazy.

My son came home from the service and he had gotten married, so I gave him my apartment. He got up one morning and he said, "Mother, what's the matter with that bird? It's just worried us to death!" He went out and threw rocks at it and everything. Well, I mentioned it to W., and said, "Do birds go crazy? I have a crazy one around here." He said he didn't know.

Well, after W. died suddenly, the bird flew away. It never happened anymore, but this happened at the time the cherries were ripe.

*Female, approximately 70, Scott County*

## Knock on the Door as Omen of Tragedy

When I was in World War II, my mother kept copious notes on my brothers and me while we were in the service. It was almost like a diary. After she died, I fell heir to her tablets. On the day on which this brother of mine was severely wounded in combat, she had written, she heard a knock on the door. She opened the door and said that she could see him just as plain as day. She felt that this was an omen.

*Male, age mid-60s, Scott County*

## A Dream and a Dove Predict Death

I dreamt before P. got killed. I dreamt it three months before it happened. Back in August, when I dreamt it, I saw a car wreck. I know it was a car wreck. And the person I saw in the wreck was C.W. It wasn't P. that got killed in my dream; it was C.W.

I seen it just as plain as day, and in the dream I run over there and C.W. was sprawled out on the ground. And I was standin' over him, wringing and rollin' my hands, and looking down at C.W. He was laying there with his eyes closed. He'd open his eyes and shut 'em. They said, "He's dead," then they'd say, "No he ain't"; first one thing, and then another.

It was a long, big dream with a whole lot in it. And after that, when August rolled around, why, then I was goin' down to Carrollton with this young woman. She worked in the public assistance office, so she came to take me down to put us on welfare. So she was drivin' this little ole car, and she turned off by the schoolhouse onto the highway there. And that grass was real green. There was a dove sittin' on the side of the highway, pickin' in at the grass. And I was kinda scared of doves; they're a kinda mopey and quiet-like bird. Anyway, she—varoom!—took off down the road, and that ole dove got up and hit the windshield just as hard! It was right on the side where I was sittin' at. And if the windshield hadda broke, why, it would have splattered me in the face.

We was talkin', but when that bird did that, I just got cold. I never said another word to her all the way to Carrollton. Then when I got home, I kept a-worryin' about it. It just kept a-worryin' me 'cause 'at bird got killed like that. And any other time, you know, it never would've bothered me. See, that was a token letting me know that something was gonna happen. I knew somethin' was gonna happen, but I didn't know what, and who, 'cause it never revealed P. to me, like, right out, you know.

I would lay in bed at night, and I'd try not to think about it. It'd just pop in my mind; it'd be on my mind. I'd think about C.W., but it just never would stay on to P. It went on until October. When October rolled around, sho'nuff P. got killed. They hit head-on, when P. got killed, just like that bird.

*Female, age 60, Carroll County*

## Loud Noise Signifies Death

I was in the bathroom washing my teeth, and something just fell in the furnace room. It was just like everything had crashed in there, you know. I went and looked, and there wasn't a thing that had fallen (nothing *to* fall, you see). About a half an hour later, I got the word that B. was dead. Token of his death, I thought it was.

*Female, age 70, Scott County*

# Chills Before Death

I was about ten years old when me and my brothers and a bunch of cousins went over to my granddaddy and grandmama's house. We were always doing something together back then, and we usually went over to the big house; that's where they live, my granddaddy and grandmama.

We got over there and was goofing around. Then we decided we all wanted to spend the night because we always got to sleep together in the attic. It was almost our bedtime when all of a sudden Mama started getting these cold chills. At first she thought someone was walking on her grave, but the chills kept coming. We started to go up the steps when she yelled at us to get ready to leave. We didn't want to go, so we kind of stood around. Then she got really mad and practically drug us out of the house. All she said to Granddaddy and Grandmama was that she wanted us kids to stay with her that night.

After we got home, we went to bed. About 2:00 in the morning, the phone rang, so I got up and answered it. It was somebody wanting to talk to Mama. They wouldn't tell me who they were. Mama talked to them for awhile, then she said she had to leave.

She wouldn't tell us anything, so we started to cry because we thought something had happened to Daddy, because he's a doctor and was at the hospital. Some neighbor lady came over and stayed till the next morning. Mama came home and told us Granddaddy and Grandmama's house had burnt down. She said the boiler had exploded and went straight through the attic. Both of my grandparents were killed. It was an awful thing to think that all of us would have been killed if we had stayed.

*Female, age 17, Boyle County*

# Ball of Fire Precedes Death

People knew this man was going to die, and everybody was sitting around. I don't guess they was *waiting* for him to die, but there wasn't much else to do. They said that this ball of fire just seemed to fall down and down the steps, went across the room, and rolled under this man's bed. Then, just as soon as the ball of fire rolled under his bed, he died!

*Female, age 55, Scott County*

## Three Balls of Fire

My father's dad, my grandfather, said that when Judgment Day came, there'd be a big blast of fire. My father told me, and my mother said it was true, that this happened on the night his daddy died. His daddy was healthy; he'd been out working in a field with a team of mules all day.

Anyway, that night there was a glow in the sky. They went to the window and saw a ball of fire. My dad said that when he went to the window to see it, the ball of fire would move to the left and move to the right. There it split up into three different parts.

When the three parts came back together, my grandfather died. My dad said that he had been told years ago that when judgment came, there would be three angels. He didn't know if that's what it was, or if it was just a freak accident that the three balls came together in the yard at the same time, or what. But my grandfather died right then.

*Male, age mid-30s, Henry County*

## Superstition About Funerals

If you have a pet house cat then it will leave the household right before a death in the household, and he will return when the funeral and things are over.

*Male, age unknown, Scott County*

## "Bird in House" Death Omen

Death omens . . . Let me see. . . . I suppose you've heard the one about a bird flying into your house. Yeah, that's one.

*Female, age 50, Fayette County*

# Death Follows Appearance of Bird

I don't have no ghost stories, but there was once when we came back from summer vacation and there was this bird in the house. The next day my grandmother died. Too, my grandmother had been in the house no more than two weeks prior to that.

*Male, age 50, Fayette County*

# Pictures as Death and Sickness Omens

They say a picture falling off the wall is a death omen. One hanging crooked is a sign of sickness. I don't pay no attention to them crazy things though.

*Female, age 60, Scott County*

# Insect Death Omen

A cricket in the house is good luck, and people used to keep crickets in small cages on the hearth for that reason. However, if the cricket leaves a home after living there for a while, it is considered to be an omen of death.

*Male, age 50, Harrison County*

# Trouble Out of Reason

You know the old superstition "Things out of season, trouble out of reason." Well, that's an old one; my mother used to say it. For example, if she'd find a rose blooming in the early winter or sometime when it shouldn't be, she would say, "Things out of season, trouble out of reason," which meant, of course, someone was going to die, or maybe many people.

Well, the only ghost story that I know happened to me and to someone that I liked very much. We had been coming home from the county seat, and he told me that he had felt as if there were a dark shadow coming up toward him, in back of him, and that he felt that he was going to have some terrible trouble. He talked about it.

Well, we went to a square dance not long after that, and it was a moonlit night. And as we were returning home, we were walking by a rock wall, and we weren't saying anything. It was quiet, and as I said, the moon was shining very brightly. By the side of the road—I could have reached out and touched him—there was a man standing there, and this man *was* the person I was with. In other words, he was walking with me *and* he was standing over there, too, in the bright moonlight.

And I said to him, after we'd walked on a little distance, "Did you see what I saw?"

He said, "Yes I did," and I could tell that he was moved by it (or whatever the word might be). I said, "Who was it?"

He said, "It was me." Well, um, it was a very strange experience. We went on home.

Then a little later in the fall, we walked across the hills, over another creek to church. We walked great distances to church; it was just a lot of fun. And we had topped the ridge and started down on the other side, and he said, "Wait for me. I'm going to walk around the hill." So I stood there and waited, and he didn't come back, and I got up and started running down the hill.

I passed him sitting beside the path, looking up at me and laughing. And I said, "I'll beat you," and I ran on down the hill. I ran as fast as I could, down over the next bluff. There he really was, standing, waiting for me in the path. I even put my hand on his heart to see if he had been running, you know, to see if he had been running to tease me, to play a trick on me, and his heart was just lazy. He hadn't been running at all.

We really felt upset about that, and that fall there was trouble out of reason in his family, a great tragedy to him and to his family.

Now that is as near as I ever had to a ghost story. And I am positive that it was no imagination, it was real, in both cases. Later, after I married, I told my husband this story, and he wrote a poem about my experience. It's called "Warning."

*Female, age mid-60s, Scott County*

# Bad Luck Omens

Here are three bad luck omens that I know:

I used to hear old people say it was bad luck to stand and watch someone out of sight.

The old folks always said that if a bird lights on your shoulder it's bad luck.

I used to hear old people say that if somebody is real sick and you hear them call your name, they won't be around too long. I dreamt, and I had this funny feeling that daddy was gonna die before I did. A week or two before he died, why, I heard him calling me one night, just as plain as I'm sittin' on this couch, and I heard him calling my name. I knew he wasn't gonna get well 'cause I heard him calling my name like that.

*Female, age 55, Carroll County*

# Considerate to the End

Aunt Josephine, who was called Penie, and her sister were the last of eleven children from an era of good manners. They were both blind and living together in a nursing home. It seems Aunt Penie raised her head one evening and said to her helper, "Do you want us to stay one more night before we go home?"

The helper said, "Yes, that would be nice." Aunt Penie said, "OK," put her head down on the pillow, and went to sleep. She died the next morning.

*Female, age 40, Fayette County*

# Notes

1. Rosemary Ellen Guiley, *The Encyclopedia of Ghosts and Spirits* (New York: Facts on File, 1992), 90.

# Chapter 10

# A Collection of Ghost Stories

The following stories were contributed to this anthology by Abigail McCormick Harris, now of Disputanta, Kentucky. She collected and wrote these accounts while in junior high school in Georgetown, demonstrating her sincere interest in the ghost lore of the Bluegrass region. There are many good ghost stories in Kentucky waiting to be collected, and even young people, equipped with a recording device and a computer, can be part of preserving this form of local history.

## The Spirited Tombstone at Federal Hill

When most people think of Federal Hill at Bardstown, Kentucky, more widely known as "My Old Kentucky Home," they usually think of Stephen Foster. But many other famous people have visited there also, such as Henry Clay, James Monroe, James K. Polk, and General Lafayette, who gave the dining room chairs that are still there. Federal Hill was built by Judge John Rowan, who started the house in 1795 and completed it in 1800. It was built in a Kentucky Georgian style. All of the rooms are square and the same size.

Judge Rowan was very accomplished, but he was a very willful, grumpy man who had an awful temper. In his will, Judge Rowan stated that he did not want a tombstone of any kind because his parents had not had one. After he died, his descendants decided that he should have a marker because he was such an important person, and they ordered an obelisk to be erected in the family cemetery. Shortly

Tombstone of Judge John Rowan, My Old Kentucky Home State Park, Bardstown, Kentucky. Note that the tombstone is leaning. (Photograph by James McCormick, permission of Kentucky Department of Parks, My Old Kentucky Home State Park, Bardstown, Kentucky.)

after it was erected, it fell down. Stonemasons came to put it back up but could find no explanation for its falling. Remembering Rowan's fiery temper—he once killed a man in a duel!—and the fact that he had wanted no tombstone, some people thought it was the judge who had knocked over the stone. When the stone fell a second time, it was almost impossible to get any men to put it back.

# Sara's Ghost

On a hill near Lake Cumberland in what is now Russell County, Kentucky, there is an old log cabin owned by my grandfather (W. G. Kirtley), who bought and restored it around 1960, and who changed its name from "Jacob's Cabin" to "Old House." The cabin was built in 1840 and was bought by the Jacob Ashley family in 1882.

Jacob Ashley owned a large area of land, Jacob's Clearing, the site of Old House. Jacob, his wife, Martha, and their daughter, Sara, lived in the cabin.

Sara Ashley was said to have what is today known as mental telepathy. She supposedly once overpowered her father's mind and made him get an axe and kill his mules. Jacob did this and returned with all of the mules' heads hanging over his shoulder.

In about 1885, Martha died. Shortly after this, Jacob awoke suddenly one night. The moon was shining in his window when suddenly he heard a voice. Quietly, then louder and louder, it said, "Kill, Kill, Kill!"

It was his daughter's voice. Quietly, Jacob grabbed the first thing in sight, his axe. Swiftly he moved toward Sara, and then he slammed the axe into her heart.

Jacob ran and ran and finally stopped in a cave to rest. About a week later, a trapper came by the cabin and saw the door open. He went in and saw the awful sight and ran out hurriedly. Sara was buried in the field next to Old House.

Over a year later, Jacob's body was found in the cave, headless, and nearby was the axe he had left in Sarah's chest in 1885! Jacob was buried beside Sara. Sara's tombstone is still there, and Jacob's grave is still visible.

My grandfather says that Sara comes to see him when a fire is going in the old stone fireplace. He says she has dark brown hair, which she wears in a knot on the back of her head. She always wears a bluish-gray dress that comes down over her feet. When Sara comes, she talks about all the children who died there and about the people who owned the Old House before my grandfather. She never stays more than five or ten minutes in one visit but may come several times a night. She showed him where the old spring was and where the children wore the stones down on the hearth.

She doesn't want my grandfather to sell the Old House because he is the only one who ever tried to keep it nice. She doesn't want him to change it. The reason, he says, that Sara haunts Old House is because she feels that she committed sins on earth, especially in Old House, and she comes to seek forgiveness.

She never appears unless my grandfather is there alone, so I've never seen her.

W. G. Kirtley sold Old House in the mid-1980s. The new owner used it as a weekend retreat but soon tired of it, and, neglected, it burned to the ground in 1990. No cause of the fire has ever been determined.

## The Gray Lady of Liberty Hall

Near the Kentucky River in Frankfort is an old Georgian house, Liberty Hall. The house was started in 1796 by John Brown, Kentucky's first senator, and was completed in 1800.

In 1799 John Brown married Margaretta Mason from New York, and he brought her to Liberty Hall. She was the daughter of a Presbyterian minister, the sister of another, and the daughter-in-law of another. She started the first Sunday School west of Pittsburgh, and she wrote the Sunday School books by hand. The books were called "Food for Lambs," and some are still to be seen at Liberty Hall. Being from New York, Margaretta was against slavery, and the Browns freed their slaves in 1820, although most people didn't free them until the 1860s.

Some time after the Browns built Liberty Hall, their daughter, Euphemia Helen Brown, died at the age of eight. The Browns were very depressed and gloomy. John retired from public office at this time, and the great ballroom was made into a hallway and a bedroom. Margaretta's sixty-five-year-old aunt, Mrs. Verrick, came to

Frankfort from New York to try to cheer them up. Only three days after she arrived, however, she had a heart attack and died, which made everyone even more sad!

Since the time of her death, members of the family have seen her in all of the rooms of the house. She has gray hair and wears a long, gray silk dress that rustles when she moves. This is why she is called the Gray Lady. Many unusual things have happened. Doors close without any wind, rocking chairs start rocking, and lights have been seen where no natural lights could be. She often came to tuck the children in bed at night.

A very interesting thing happened in 1966. It was a cold, snowy January, and no tourist had been to Liberty Hall that month. Mrs. Coleman, the curator of Liberty Hall, went into a bedroom and happened to look on the tea table and saw three thin gold bracelets. She knew there had been no tourists, and they weren't hers. Maybe they were the Gray Lady's.

Mrs. Coleman took them to a jeweler, and he determined that they had been made in New York before 1800. They are still on the table, and no one has come to claim them.

There is an actual photograph of the Gray Lady. When taking pictures for the restoration of Liberty Hall, someone took a picture of the stairs. When they developed the film, there was a definite outline of a figure on the stairs!

Many famous people have visited Liberty Hall, including Thomas Jefferson, Zachary Taylor, President Monroe, and General Lafayette, but to me one of the most interesting is the Gray Lady.

## The Helpful Ghosts of the Muddiman House

On the edge of Georgetown in Scott County, Kentucky, there is an old house that is said to be haunted. It was built in 1843 by Jefferson Craig, the nephew of Elijah Craig, founder of both Georgetown College and the Kentucky bourbon industry.

The house is now owned by the Muddiman family and is lived in by G. and her two children. It is a two-story brick house painted white, and in the backyard there are three tombstones. One of the

Liberty Hall, Frankfort, Kentucky. If you could look through the window, you might see an image of the lady on the staircase. (Photograph courtesy of Liberty Hall Historic Home, Frankfort, Kentucky.)

unusual happenings at the Muddiman house concerns the tombstone of Martin Hawkins, who died in 1830. (He is not buried there, but his tombstone is there, which is also unusual.) The tombstone is of an old style that is placed flat on the ground. G. told me, "We have noticed in the three years we have lived here that no matter how much snow or ice is on the ground, the part of the tombstone with his name on it is hardly ever covered, but the rest of it is!" One day I went there when it was snowing and the name was covered. But another snowy, icy day I went and all but the name was covered.

Two people have committed suicide in the Muddiman house, a man, Henry Craig, and a young woman. Persons who have previously lived in the house said that if you put a box of powder on the dresser, sometimes the form of a man and a woman would rise up out of it.

During Christmas, G. and her family had a Christmas tree. One night G. was ready to go to bed, so she told her daughter to turn off the tree lights. The second after she told her to turn them off, they went out. Her daughter wasn't even close to the tree! Then G. said she had better see what had happened to the lights and started toward the tree. The second after she said that, the lights flashed back on.

G. said that the first time she got the idea there were spirits in the house was when she first moved in. The floor was very dirty, and so she scrubbed it. When she came back after letting it dry, however, all of the tiles had come loose and were curled up and out of place. They talked about what kind of paste to get to put the tiles back down, then G. went to buy the paste. But when she came back to paste them down, the tiles were all glued and back in place!

G. and her family feel that the spirits are not harmful or threatening in any way, although at times they do get a bit spooked at the thought of having a ghost around.

*Chapter 11*

# A Ghost Story from the Nineteenth Century

T he following is an account of the strange occurrences that beset the Horrell family, as recorded in a small book with a long title, *A Short Statement Concerning the Strange Visitation Which During Twenty Nine Years, Afflicted THE FAMILY OF JOHN HORRELL, Living near St. Anthony's Church, Long Lick, Breckinridge Co., Ky.,* by J. J. Abell. This book was loaned to us by Mrs. Tillie Moore of Lexington, Kentucky, who found the book in an antique shop in the Old Frankfort Avenue area of Louisville, Kentucky. After we searched online and in the OCLC WorldCat,[1] it became apparent that this is one of the few surviving copies of Abell's book, and for this reason, and because it fits the ghost story genre, it is included, unedited, in its entirety. It is a most unusual story, violent, and ending on a vulgar note as if to emphasize the depravity of the poltergeists and apparitions involved. It is a modest publication in size, measuring 7½ by 5½ inches, and it is fifteen pages long. The story is written in extremely long, very inclusive paragraphs. The language and social implications are those of the times.

J. J. Abell states, "I never had the opportunity to obtain a statement of facts till August 22, 1875." He interviewed his grandmother, father, uncle, and his grandfather's pastor about the events that began "sometime during the year 1838."

The book does not seem to be an attempt at fiction in the nineteenth-century mode of Horace Walpole or Mary Shelley. Read it and decide for yourselves.

A Short Statement

Concerning the Strange Visitation Which During Twenty Nine Years, Afflicted

## THE FAMILY OF JOHN HORRELL,

### Living near St. Anthony's Church, Long Lick, Breckinridge Co., Ky.

## GRANDMOTHER'S STATEMENT

In childhood days, I heard my parents, and near relatives, now and then speak guardedly of a series of mysterious events that once took place in Breckinridge Co., Ky. at the residence of my grandfather, John Horrell. Seldom was any reference made to those strange occurrences, since discussion of them could only serve to bring the family into publicity, in connection with matters of unpleasant memory. Owing to the unwillingness of my grandfather's family to speak upon the subject, I never had opportunity to obtain a definite statement of facts, until Aug. 22, 1875, during a visit to my venerable grandmother. Her testimony was substantially as follows:

Sometime during the year 1838, the attention of the family was first drawn to queer occurrences about their premises. These happenings, at first few, and barely peculiar enough to deserve notice, gradually increased in number and strangeness as time wore on, till they became the wonder of the neighborhood. Every kind of mischief was wrought. Clothes unaccountably disappeared from the places where they were usually kept. Sometimes they were found, long afterward, lying out in the open fields, partially or wholly ruined by exposure to the weather. Again, they were found about the house, thrust into all manner of out-of-the-way holes and corners. Mr. Horrell, in common with other early settlers, did his own shoe making and cobbling. For such purposes, he kept a supply of leather on hand. A portion of it disappeared most unaccountably. Two of the children, passing one day through the lane, a quarter-mile from the house, found the missing leather, all cut into little pieces. On the ground, near by, lay a table knife with which apparently, the cutting had been done. The stirrup-leather of Mrs. Horrell's side-saddle was found cut in two—and close to each other, in the thick flap running around the saddle-bow, there were four or five gashes cut about a quarter of an inch deep. Towels were found cut to pieces, or punched through with numerous holes that looked as if they had been made with a sharp-pointed scissors. Fine coverlets folded and laid away in drawers, when next inspected, were frequently found cut or pierced in the same manner, so that Mrs. Horrell finally placed the unmutilated ones in her mother's keeping, where they remained unmolested. Late one evening, Mr. Horrell brought home from the store a bolt of factory cotton. It was placed in a bureau drawer till morning, when upon unrolling it, Mrs. Horrell found it so gashed and cut that there remained no piece as large as a handkerchief. As time wore on, even the domestic animals were tampered with. The cows, for instance, were milked, and the geese picked by an unknown agency. Indeed, the inexplicable picking of the geese happened occasionally till the later part of the year 1867, when the family finally moved away from the farm. One day, Mrs. Horrell, preparing dinner, lifted the cover of the "oven" to see how her bread was baking. She found sunk into the dough a rusty, dirty tin cup, that had long since been worn out and thrown away. Another day, an old grease-brush, used for smearing tallow on shoes, was found in the middle of a "pone" of bread when it was cut open at meal time. This bread was prepared and baked under the watchful eye of Mrs. Horrell herself. At length, the power of this malevolent agent extended even to the children, who were the first, and (with possibly a single exception) the only persons, to whom it ever became visible. *See Note A.* They were tormented in many ways, and united in testifying that it was sometimes an old woman,—other times an old man who harassed them. According to their childish description, the man, or woman, or thing was black and nearly always accompanied by a large black dog, marked with yellow spots. The children often saw the dog and its master, but neither Mr. nor Mrs. Horrell caught sight of them. Frequently, one or other of the children, at play out doors, would be heard screaming, and found running toward the house in extreme terror. When questioned as to the cause of its fright, it would answer that an "Old Black Woman," or "Man" had chased it. One day, when Mrs. Horrell and her mother, Margaret Rhodes, were engaged in the kitchen, Tom, a child of four or five years, who had just been playing around the door, ran in entirely naked. Mrs. Rhodes instantly rushed outdoors and around the house with the purpose of catching sight of the one who had stripped the boy, but saw no sign of any person or thing unusual about the premises. Search was then made for the child's clothes, but without success. After some months, these clothes, ruined by exposure to the weather, were found wadded together and thrust into a crevice between the chimney and the house, ten or fifteen feet from the ground. *See Note B.* In order to accommodate some visitor, three or four of the little girls gave up their bedroom one evening, and occupied pallets in the sleeping apartment of their parents. That night a scream from Mary, the eldest girl, aroused the household. Upon examination, it was found that a whole handful of her hair had been plucked out, leaving a raw place on her scalp, which became very sore. A thorough search failed to show any trace of the missing hair. Occasionally, one of the children would run into the house from play, extremely frightened, with its clothes sometimes torn, sometimes cut, literally in strips. Other times, one of them might be heard screaming and seen struggling, evidently in the greatest distress. Father or mother, rushing to the rescue, would find the child's face livid, and finger marks on its throat, as if some one had just been choking it. Mary and Teresa, the two eldest girls, were again and again caught up and thrown back and forth over a rail fence six rails high. One of the little boys, on one occasion, was dragged across the yard, thrust into a horse trough full of water and held there, despite his struggles, till he was almost drowned. Whenever the children suffered personal violence, as in the cases just cited, those who rescued them, however promptly, never saw "The Old Black Man" or "Woman" who, according to the terrified little sufferers was their persecutor, and who, they said, ran away when any one came in response to their cries for help.

Occurrences similar to those above related took place almost daily for many years. Careful watches were often kept by the family or neighbors, with a view of solving the mystery, but always without success. The mischief continued during periods of vigilance without change,—except that it became possibly more malignant on such occasions. *See Note C.* Father Degauquier, the pastor of that congregation, was consulted. He "went about over the premises saying prayers" and twice celebrated the Holy Sacrifice in the house. The Sisters of Loretto made Novenas. Still the trouble continued without interruption, as much defiant of spiritual as of material aids invoked against it. And so, for years, that devoted family, with Christian fortitude and patience, endured an affliction comparable in kind, if not in degree, with that suffered by Job. At length the activity of the unknown power diminished. The mysterious occurrences gradually grew less frequent and less annoying. Finally, they all together ceased about the year 1853, with the exception that the geese were occasionally found picked, during the following fourteen years, as noted above. The cause of the origin, continuance and ending of the preternatural events, remained an unfathomed mystery.

*(Signed) J.J. Abell*

## Note A—Crutchelo's Adventure

Reverend John A. Barrett was my grandfather's pastor for some years about 1865. He made a strong effort to clear up the mystery of the Horrell home, trying particularly to find out whether any one, besides the children, had seen the "black person." As far as Father Barrett could ascertain, no one else ever saw anything, except Mr. Crutchelo, a near neighbor. This man was an expert with the rifle and very fond of fox-chasing. He scouted the idea that other than human agency was responsible for the mischief wrought at the Horrell house, and privately held Mr. Horrell's skill and penetration in light esteem because of his failure to detect the guilty party. One evening, Mr. Horrell came to Crutchelo and after explaining that himself and his wife were summoned to Hardinsburg on pressing business, begged his neighbor to protect the children during their

absence the following day. Crutchelo willingly assented, and early
the next morning came over, mounted on his fleetest hunting horse,
carrying his rifle and accompanied by his pack of fox-hounds, the
best in the County. After the departure of Mr. and Mrs. Horrell,
Crutchelo threw open every gateway leading out from the house,
brought his horse into the yard, and placing a chair under a shade-
tree whence a clear view of the grounds could be maintained, seated
himself with rifle across his knees, horse on one side and hounds
on the other. Then, having directed the children to play as usual
about the yard, but to remain always within sight, he devoted his
trained eye and ear to the task of solving the mystery. After some
hours of watching, one of the children screamed in terror, and at
that moment Crutchelo saw what seemed a black woman running
with incredible swiftness from the children toward the yard fence.
Instantly, the hounds were in hot pursuit, following eagerly their
strange chase over a six rail fence and across the precipitous ravine of
the spring branch to a road leading from the house up Rough Creek.
Meantime, Crutchelo sprang into his saddle, galloped through the
open gates around the head of the ravine, and joined his hounds
in their fierce pursuit. Swiftly as the hounds ran, they did not gain
on the fleeing object. After some five hundred yards had been covered, dogs and hunter straining every nerve without lessening the
distance between themselves and the thing, it suddenly put forth a
terrific speed that quickly carried it away from horse and hounds and
out of sight, around a bend of the road. Then Crutchelo thought of
the children left without protection, and galloped back to the house
where he found them badly frightened, but safe. He could still hear
the hounds, but they were no longer in full cry, and seemed to have
lost the trail and to be vainly trying to recover it. After Mr. and
Mrs. Horrell's return, Crutchelo, with a hunter's instinct, examined
the dust road for tracks, and found them—made by a naked human
foot and measuring from one to the next, THE PRODIGIOUS DIS-
TANCE OF 18 to 20 FEET!!

The above was related to me by Father Barrett.

*(Signed) J. J. Abell*

## Note B—Instance of Hidden Money

During the reign of mischief at Grandfather's, Ben Horrell, his half-brother, came one Christmas to visit the family. Great was the welcome accorded him. Fresh logs were thrown upon the roaring fire by some of the family, while others assisted in removing his great coat, which they hung upon a hook on the wall,—then a wide circle was formed about the fireplace with Uncle Ben in the place of honor, but almost immediately their joy was checked by a weird occurrence,—for suddenly, the great coat, carefully hung up a moment before, was seen to jump from the hook,—sail through the air overhead to about the center of the room, where it whirled rapidly round for a few seconds, and at last dropped out-spread on the floor. Uncle Ben picked up his coat, put it on, and remarking that he would go on to Frank Rhodes's, remounted his horse and rode away. After a short time, however, he returned and informed my grandfather that a leather purse containing about twenty dollars had been in an inner pocket of the overcoat when he first arrived, but was then missing. A thorough search for the purse or money was fruitlessly made, and, to my grandfather's mortification, Uncle Ben had to leave without his money. The following spring, while giving the house a general cleaning, my grandmother had occasion to overhaul and dust some odds and ends stowed away on the top shelf of her three-cornered cupboard. In the farthest corner of the shelf was a cracked teacup she had placed there herself a year before. When she lifted it, she found underneath Ben Horrell's purse, still containing the exact sum he said was in it at the time of its disappearance.

The above was related to me by my father, who got the account from my mother and from Ben Horrell himself.

*(Signed) J. J. Abell*

## Note C—Specially Malicious When Watched

One day, when the trouble was at its worst, Margaret Rhodes visited her daughter—Mrs. Horrell. While dinner was cooking, Mrs.

Rhodes undertook to make the bread, with a strong determination to prevent any intrusion into it of such filth as the mischievous power overshadowing the house was frequently pleased to convey into the daily food of the family. Having personally prepared the bread, and placed it in the "oven," she seated herself hard by and watched it continuously, never allowing her eyes to wander. When she lifted the lid of the "oven" in order to note the progress of baking, to her amazement she found, neatly deposited upon the baking bread a FRESH HUMAN EXCREMENT!

The above was related to me by my uncle, E. R. Horrell, the eldest son of John Horrell.

*(Signed) J. J. Abell*

# Notes

1. OCLC WorldCat is a meta search engine for the online catalogs of tens of thousands of libraries all over the world. See "About OCLC," at http://www.oclc.org/about/default.htm (accessed December 17, 2008).

# Conclusion

We are grateful to the many people who have contributed to this anthology, especially the students whose work formed the nucleus of this collection. It is apparent that the oral tradition of ghost and death lore is still alive in our culture today. While we have made no attempt to prove or disprove the truthfulness of the stories herein, we acknowledge that ghost stories are an integral part of our heritage and should not be ignored. The stories presented here for the most part are from Kentucky. After reading and researching stories from other regions of the United States, however, we recognized a strong similarity in themes. This is also true of death lore.

Why do different people, in different locations and times, see similar ghosts? The "vanishing hitchhiker" is one example of a widespread, almost clichéd, ghost, about which stories are continually passed down through generations and across cultures. Does the fact that this ghost type is reported so very often simply indicate that it is a universally appealing form of ghost lore? Or is it so widespread because there are many of these sorts of ghosts around? Regardless of where and when they died, people who die a certain type of death perhaps tend to become ghosts, doomed to continue their interrupted journey, and are thus more likely to be encountered than are people who die in less distressing ways.

At the beginning of our story-collecting project, the writers approached the subject with enthusiasm tempered with skepticism. This attitude still prevails, but with perhaps a healthy dose of enlightenment added. There is no doubt that some people are more sensitive to the supernatural than others, but why this is so remains a mystery. Hearing people describe their ghostly experiences makes one realize that, whether or not supernatural phenomena exist, they are undoubtedly real in the minds of those who have had these experiences and who shared their stories. Skepticism is healthy, but one has to be careful to also keep an open mind and not let initial beliefs block evidence that might be presented at a later date. One also has to be careful to not simply look for evidence that confirms what one already believes and to ignore evidence that contradicts that belief. And, it became clear to us, one also has to be careful to review all the information presented and to process that information as logically as possible, even when presented with information that defies logic!

Our research on those who have attempted to film ghosts or spirits made clear that it is often very difficult to do. However, among our sources there were several mentions of ghosts being captured on film. The Old Fort Harrod State Park ghost had, according to one storyteller, been seen on film negatives. Dr. Funkhouser, the University of Kentucky professor discussed in chapter 8, appears in a photo owned by the teller of "Scholar Reappears," and the "Gray Lady of Liberty Hall" (chapter 10) is apparently not shy of the camera, either. Another storyteller did not actually take a picture of her ghost, but one theory she put forth was that the image at the window (see chapter 1) was a sort of photographic image left on the window glass out of which the old lady looked for many years before her death. Were these images captured on film really floating ectoplasm or simply dust? With the advent of computer photo editing capabilities, photographic evidence is going to become less and less reliable as any sort of proof. (UFO sighters have the same issues to contend with, although photos of purported UFOs are abundant.) Unfortunately, we were unable to examine any of the photos mentioned in this anthology ourselves.

Of note is the fact that the stories came not only from people of all educational backgrounds, but from people of all age groups as well. Many young people reported a ghost or death omen experience. This indicates that the ghost story is not a dying tradition, but one that is still with us. At one time ghosts rode horses and carriages; now they occupy Pontiacs and listen to the radio. It appears that collecting the ghost story is a never-ending endeavor.

The most interesting finding, and what is most striking, is that practically every person approached and asked for an interview had a ghost story to tell. If the event had not happened to the person being interviewed, it had, in many cases, happened to someone he knew, and it had impressed him enough to be remembered and retold to one of our participants. It seems evident that ghost stories are of universal interest because they deal with the unknown, which is so elusive it tickles our curiosity and tempts us to delve further into it.

Do ghosts exist? The authors of this anthology hope our stories have whetted your appetite, and that some readers will be moved to follow up with further research. If you have more questions now than you did when you started this book, then we have achieved one of our goals in writing it.

We hope you have enjoyed reading this collection of ghost stories and death lore, and that the tales did not disrupt your sleep. We leave you with a word of caution: when you hear something go bump in the night, ask yourself, "Is it *really* just the wind?"

# Bibliography

Bondeson, Jan. *Buried Alive: The Terrifying History of Our Most Primal Fear*. New York: W. W. Norton, 2001.

Brunvand, Jan Harold. *The Vanishing Hitchhiker*. New York: W. W. Norton, 1981.

Danelek, J. Allan. *The Case for Ghosts*. Woodbury, Minn.: Llewellyn Publications, 2006.

Goodman, Felicitas. *How About Demons?* Bloomington: Indiana University Press, 1988.

Guiley, Rosemary Ellen. *The Encyclopedia of Ghosts and Spirits*. New York: Facts on File, 1992.

Kallen, Stuart A. *Ghosts*. Farmington Hills, Mich.: Lucent Books, 2004.

Molin, Charles. *Ghosts, Spooks and Spectors*. New York: David White, 1967.

Norman, Michael, and Beth Scott. *Haunted Heritage*. New York: Tom Doherty Associates, 2002.

Ramsland, Katherine. *Ghosts: Investigating the Other Side*. New York: Thomas Dunne Books, 2001.

Thompson, Stith. *Motif-Index of Folk-Literature*. Bloomington: Indiana University Press, 1989.

## Suggested Readings

Ashley, Leonard R. N. *The Complete Book of Ghosts and Poltergeists*. New York: Barricade Books, 2000.

Bennett, Gillian. *Alas, Poor Ghost!* Logan: Utah State University Press, 1999.

Cavendish, Richard. *The World of Ghosts and the Supernatural*. New York: Facts on File, 1994.

185

Clarke, Kenneth, and Mary Clarke. *The Harvest and the Reapers*. Lexington: University Press of Kentucky, 1974.

Crowe, Catherine. *The Night Side of Nature*. Wellingborough, U.K.: Aquarian Press, 1986.

Degh, Linda. *People in the Tobacco Belt: Four Lives*. Ottawa: National Museums of Canada, 1975.

Finucane, R. C. *Appearances of the Dead: A Cultural History of Ghosts*. London: Junction Books, 1982.

Gauld, Alan, and A. D. Cornell. *Poltergeists*. London: Routledge and Kegan Paul, 1979.

Haining, Peter. *Ghosts: The Illustrated History*. Secaucus, N.J.: Chartwell Books, 1988.

Holland, Jeffrey S. *Weird Kentucky*. New York: Sterling, 2008.

Holzer, Hans. *Ghosts: True Encounters with the World Beyond*. New York: Black Dog and Leventhal, 1997.

Hubbard, Sylvia Booth. *Ghosts! Personal Accounts of Modern Mississippi Hauntings*. Brandon, Miss.: Quail Ridge Press, 1992.

Hufford, David J. *The Terror That Comes in the Night: An Experience-Centered Study of Supernatural Assault Tradition*. Philadelphia: University of Pennsylvania Press, 1982.

Hurston, Zora Neale. *Folklore, Memoirs, and Other Writings*. New York: Penguin Books, 1995.

Montell, William L. *Ghosts across Kentucky*. Lexington: University Press of Kentucky, 2000.

———. *Ghosts along the Cumberland*. Knoxville: University of Tennessee Press, 1975.

———. *Haunted Houses and Family Ghosts of Kentucky*. Lexington: University Press of Kentucky, 2001.

Musick, Ruth Ann. *Coffin Hollow and Other Ghost Stories*. Lexington: University Press of Kentucky, 1977.

Osborne-Thomason, Natalie. *The Ghost Hunting Casebook*. Bodmin, Cornwall: MPG Books, 1999.

Oscard, Anne. *Tri-state Terrors: Famous Ghosts of Ohio, Indiana and Kentucky*. Dayton, Ohio: Hermit Publications, 1996.

Owens, A. R. G. *Can We Explain the Poltergeist?* New York: Helix, 1964.

Roberts, Leonard W. *South from Hell-fer-Sartin*. Lexington: University Press of Kentucky, 1955.

Seymour, St. John D., and Harry L. Neligan. *True Irish Ghost Stories*. New York: Causeway, 1974.

Tucker, Elizabeth. *Haunted Halls: Ghostlore of American College Campuses*. Jackson: University Press of Mississippi, 2007.

Van Praagh, James. *Ghosts among Us: Uncovering the Truth about the Other Side*. New York: HarperOne, 2008.

Warren, Joshua P. *Pet Ghosts: Animal Encounters from Beyond the Grave*. Franklin Lakes, N.J.: New Page Books, 2006.

Young, Richard, and Judy D. Young. *Ozark Ghost Stories*. Little Rock, Ark.: August House, 1995.